A Drama of Reform

A DRAMA OF REFORM

BENEDICT GROESCHEL, C.F.R.

and

THE FRANCISCANS OF THE RENEWAL

Photography by

GRAZYNA MARCZUK

IGNATIUS PRESS

SAN FRANCISCO

Cover art:
Crucifix of San Damiano
Anonymous, 13th century
S. Chiara, Assisi, Italy
© Scala / Art Resource, New York

Front cover photograph by Grazyna Marczuk
Back cover photograph by Rosann Mucciolo

Cover design by Roxanne Mei Lum

ISBN 978-1-58617-114-8
ISBN 1-58617-114-3
Library of Congress Control Number 2005926540
Printed in Canada ∞

To our Blessed Lady of Guadalupe

patroness of our community

we dedicate this book

with filial affection

Contents

Acknowledgments

I am deeply grateful to all who cooperated in bringing this book to completion. The photographs by Grazyna Marczuk were the occasion for writing the book, and we wish to acknowledge the contributions of Luc Adrian, as well.

My sincere thanks go to Father Glenn Sudano, C.F.R., our community Servant (superior), for supporting this work all along, and to Father Richard Roemer, C.F.R., Vicar of the community, who did much of the collating and assembling of the material. I am also very grateful to the Friars and Sisters who contributed their thoughts and experiences with such personal sincerity. Grateful thanks go also to my associate Charles Pendergast for his valuable assistance, and to Father Joseph Fessio, S.J., and all at Ignatius Press for their help in making this project a reality.

— Father Benedict J. Groeschel, C.F.R.

St. Crispin's Friary

February 11, 2005
Feast of Our Lady of Lourdes

APRIL 2, 1987:
Group of founding friars on the day they notified the Capuchins of their intentions.

Preface

Father Glenn Sudano, C.F.R.
Community Servant

It is with a deep sense of gratitude to God that we happily present this book to you. Some of you are family members, friends, and benefactors who have been with us from our early years. Others, perhaps, have only heard of the "CFRs", or Gray Friars, and know us from afar. Here, then, is an opportunity for us to share with you a wonderful drama, which is still unfolding.

When standing beside some ancient monastic orders, such as the Benedictines or Carthusians, we Gray Friars are rather insignificant. When compared to the robust apostolic and influential religious societies, such as the Jesuits or Salesians, we are very weak and spindly indeed. Church historians might well be quick to point out that the ink is still moist on the first page of our chronicle; while others in time-tested communities might wonder whether we are actually seaworthy. These latter may strike a let's-see posture, watching from a distance to see whether we survive the high seas, being only at the start of a voyage.

By the grace of God, the Franciscan Friars of the Renewal came to birth almost twenty years ago, in the spring of 1987, which was, providentially for us, a Marian year. That year, eight finally professed Franciscans (I being one of them) began a renewal at a time in history and with a vision that were quite similar to those of our Capuchin confreres in sixteenth-century Italy. We have much to say about—and, indeed, a debt of gratitude to offer—Pope John Paul II, who was a source of instruction and inspiration to us. If we survive the storms to come, one reason will be the strength of his Christian witness and the ballast of his wisdom and devotion.

History attests that, in every age, attempts to bring renewed vigor and focus to religious life have met with a predictable amount of fear and distrust. Times of reform are often dramatic and accompanied by the clashing of opposing ideas and expectations. The opening chapters of both the Capuchin and Carmelite reforms were not lacking in strong characters who wrestled with serpentine subplots. Understandably, to examine every aspect of our own early days would be an indiscretion. Despite the human backdrop, we should not become distracted but center our attention on the drama unfolding on center stage. No doubt, one can be both surprised and inspired, and at times perhaps entertained, by the mysterious interplay between divine grace and human weakness. Any authentic attempt to bring reform and renewal to an institution is accompanied by pain. Timid attempts to make life better rarely bring effective results. Planes never lift off the ground at low speeds, regardless of the sincere intentions of pilot or passengers. In another metaphor: tepid water makes weak tea.

Unlike us and our Capuchin forefathers, many religious communities enter the world quietly and unannounced, like spring crocuses. It often happens that a prophetic or charismatic founder or foundress sees a need in the Church or the world and personally responds to that need. Soon, others follow, and a community is formed. With us it was different. We can point to no founder, although spiritual leadership was far from lacking. Unlike many communities, we were not slowly and meticulously built, but rather quietly conceived and painfully born. Like human life, some religious communities often come into existence only by expending considerable blood, sweat, and tears. Communities of reform are indeed breech babies, who bring pain to the mother during their birth. To the uninitiated, the entire event resembles an unfortunate amputation; yet in reality it is the fortunate arrival of new life.

The Franciscan Order, begun eight centuries ago, can best be compared to an old tree: it has deep roots and diverse branches. Its history accounts for the various types of Franciscans, who have emerged over the years, each identified by a different cut and color. One of the tree's larger branches came into existence in the early sixteenth century, an era ripe for change. Members of the Franciscan reform movement, which emphasized evident material poverty, contemplative prayer, evangelical preaching, and care of the very poor, became known as the Capuchins, a nickname given by the people because of the friars' long, pointed capuche, or hood. It is from this noble and holy branch that we owe our identity and existence. In a symbolic return to the early Franciscans who wore poor, undyed wool, we changed the color of our habit from the familiar coffee-colored habit of the cappuccino to the original gray. To this day, Franciscans in England are known as Grayfriars.

When I first entered Franciscan life more than twenty-five years ago, I was like many novices: idealistic but perhaps somewhat unrealistic in my hopes for a more authentic and vibrant expression of our life. Being young, I had high ideals and a hunger for something more, something greater. Unfortunately, spiritual immaturity often draws our attention to heroic and dramatic things, such as radical poverty, and less to more important things, such as humility and charity. Now that I am older, I too smile inwardly at the innocent naïveté of the postulant who wonders why the friars don't go barefoot through the city streets and beg their food door to door.

Yet at the core of it all there rests something good—in fact, something quite beautiful. Surely, when we hold within ourselves some high ideal or great dream we may find ourselves alone, feeling odd and isolated, even from family. I remember describing myself to my spiritual director as being like a sailor standing on the deck of a large ship and pointing excitedly toward an enticing island on the horizon. The older, more seasoned sailors remained unmoved or even laughed, saying that the island was either abandoned or impossible to reach. Some said it was not real, but a mirage. Thankfully, I was not alone in what I was seeing and deeply desiring, though from a great distance. By myself I would not have found the strength to leave a secure ocean liner for a flimsy eight-man lifeboat. As I look back, it is not surprising that so few of our confreres openly praised our courage, while some quietly questioned our mental health.

By God's design and the assistance of friends like John Cardinal O'Connor, archbishop of New York, and saints like Mother Teresa, we found ourselves safely on the shores of the South Bronx. As some say, we hit the road running, because we immediately rolled up our sleeves and began to work. We weren't aware of the many obstacles ahead of us, but, thanks be to God, youthful ignorance and enthusiasm are helpful in surmounting big hurdles. Almost every day we had to deal with new situations and unanswered questions as we made our humble outpost a home in an almost abandoned and drug-infested neighborhood.

Most days were spent scraping, stripping, pulling up, and tearing up—

we call it Capuchinizing—getting rid of the old, ugly, unnecessary things such as paneling, rugs, and wallpaper. The rectory parlor became our chapel almost as soon as the tabernacle replaced the television. All the old air-conditioning units were put curbside, to the delight of local drug addicts. Somehow, in the midst of our manual labor, we found the time for so much more. Most important, we prayed, although during the summer months we were serenaded outside our chapel windows by police sirens and ungodly "music." In the midst of this we managed to serve the homeless, counsel drug addicts, and teach the children who found their way to our door. No doubt it was God who not only gave us the vision to see our Shangri-la in the distance but also brought us there safe and sound, as if carried in the palm of His hand.

From day one, our desire was not to create a new form of religious life or observance but rather to set ourselves securely upon our own ancient foundations. For this very reason, none of the original eight Friars of the Renewal see themselves as founders. We do not see ourselves as prophetic architects but rather as simple builders. In this regard, renewal does not mean some new spin on Franciscan life, nor is it an innovative amalgam of religious traditions. Rather it means a return—not simply going back, but something deeper—a return to roots. We were and still remain completely uninterested in programs and trendy ideas that promise spiritual renewal. Real renewal means daily conversion, and this is a long, painful road. The holy Gospels are our map, the saints are our guides, and the sacraments are our strength for the journey.

Our community began in 1987 with eight friars; today we number more than ninety. While, certainly, steady growth and expansion are impressive, they are not everything. The strength of a tree is not measured only by the width of its trunk or length of its limbs but also by its roots. The quality of vocations is more important than quantity, yet both are related. Both depend on the soil in which they are set. Religious life will not only survive but will flourish when it is firmly planted in the heart of Christ, who is the heart of the Church. This means nothing less than: a clear identity, total fidelity, ardent devotion, daily prayer, and sacrificial service, especially to the poor. This is what young people are seeking. This is the secret for any community intent on authentic renewal. Young eyes need to see something bright and beautiful. How sad when their longings and excitement are met with indifference and unbelief.

I pray that this book may touch your heart and the hearts of those you love. I pray its pictures may speak more than a million words, while the words of the friars and sisters "paint" something beautiful in your heart. I hope this simple work may encourage the laity, inspire the clergy, and challenge the religious. This is not a book about heroes or saints but about young people who have taken a stand, left what was safe and secure, and courageously followed their dream. It is a book that weaves God's grace with human hope, creating a stunning tapestry that tells a dramatic story of God's goodness.

As an artist steps back a bit to see how his work is taking shape, so too this book has personally provided for me a needed distance, a certain space, to see a wonderful divine work still in progress. Like poor peasants who live in the foothills of the Alps, all of us can become oblivious to something grand and majestic in our own backyard. Would that each of us might have such a book as this one to help us take a few steps back—to see what God is quietly accomplishing in our lives. May He be praised.

FALL 1987:
First community retreat as a new group.
St. Joseph's Abbey, Spencer, Massachusetts

Introduction

Benedict Groeschel, C.F.R.

A Drama of Reform is the story of the first two decades of a reform in religious life attempted in 1987 by a few Americans, most of them quite young. We were united in the desire to be authentic disciples of Jesus Christ, following in the footsteps of Saint Francis, despite our all-too-human weaknesses. As the third decade of our existence approaches, we feel moved to tell our story. We want to encourage the army of Christians of all denominations who are discouraged by the erosion of Gospel values in our culture. We are also explicit in our intention of letting other men and women religious know that there is a way out of the depressing confusion and decline that characterize most religious orders in Europe and in the English-speaking world. This way was indicated several times by Pope John Paul II.

We have used photos and short essays by members of the two independent communities of the Franciscan Friars of the Renewal and Franciscan Sisters of the Renewal in the hope that others will be able to experience the earnestness and enthusiasm of this young and fervent group. More than one hundred sisters and friars from a dozen different countries are now united by the desire to follow the Gospel of Jesus Christ after the example of Saint Francis and the tradition of the Capuchin reform.

Why do we call this story a drama? It is not because each day is dramatic but rather because there have been many dangers, many moments when, considering the difficulty of the task, we could have given up. As in every good drama, there have been beautiful days when God's blessings could be seen coming upon us, and more beautiful days spent with the poor when, despite all the labor, it was obvious that this reform was a work of God. At every step of the way we have relied on God's providence to provide for us and our work with the poor; we have tried to give ourselves over to the Holy Spirit's guidance to lead us in what we were to do; and we have looked to Christ's presence as our motive and ideal. Although we made plenty of mistakes and took false steps—an experience common to all human endeavors—we could not fail to see that the Lord was with us. God's words to Joshua, as he stood at the edge of the Promised Land, often echoed in our hearts: "Be strong and of good courage; be not frightened, neither be dismayed; for the Lord your God is with you wherever you go" (Joshua 1:9).

This testimony to God's grace has two sections: first, this brief history and description of our reform; second, photographs, most with brief writings of the sisters and brothers, giving their individual experiences of the reform effort. Most of the photography was done by our friend and professional photographer Grazyna Marczuk, with occasional contributions from other professionals, such as Luc Adrian. A few snapshots, especially from the early days, are included with these introductory remarks.

The friars and sisters dedicate this book to our friends who have helped and stood by us all along the way. In particular we want to express our debt of gratitude to our now-deceased friend John Cardinal O'Connor, Archbishop of New York, who is our canonical founder, and to his assistant in charge of religious communities, Sister Catherine Quinn, P.B.V.M., who guided us so carefully and kindly in the early days. We are grateful also to the late Father Joseph Fitzpatrick, S.J., a priest and sociologist, who facilitated our meetings and gave so much help. Our community continues to enjoy the support of our benevolent Ordinary and canonical superior, Edward Cardinal Egan, who has shown paternal concern and kindness to our two communities.

We are forever in the debt of Blessed Teresa of Calcutta, whom some of us knew for thirty years and whose sisters are our neighbors in the South Bronx and Harlem. Although Mother Teresa is not responsible for our decision to begin a new community, she inspired us by the Gospel life of the Missionaries of Charity and gave us much encouragement and support from the very first day. Without her prophetic example of fervent and traditional religious life lived in the midst of a metropolis, it is doubtful that we would have attempted this reform. Shortly before we made our decision to start out, we watched the documentary movie made by Jan and Ann Petrie, titled *Mother Teresa*. A challenge presented itself clearly: If this old woman could do all this, eight able-bodied men ought to be able to do *something*.

We have also experienced the spiritual help and intercession of Saint Pio of Pietrelcina since the day we began. He is a shining example of the truth that the Capuchin reform and its unique interpretation of the way of Saint Francis still have much relevance and meaning in our confused and paganized world. To this holy apostle of charity we dedicated our first work with the poor, the Padre Pio Shelter. We were inspired also by the example of the Capuchin mystic and healer, the Venerable Solanus Casey of Detroit. His extraordinary devotion to Christ and to the poor, sick, and needy brought to my youth a shining light that has remained with me for half a century.

Why Reform?

At Padre Pio's beatification ceremony in Saint Peter's Square, a group of fervent young Capuchin friars from Slovakia came up to us when they noticed that our habits were the same as theirs with the exception of the color (ours were gray rather than brown). When Father Andrew and I explained who we were, they asked, "Why reform?" Several years later I met them again, in Slovakia, where the Catholic faith has come back to life after decades of persecution and repression and is now vibrant. Their question seemed as relevant as ever. It raises important issues.

THE CRISIS IN RELIGIOUS LIFE

As is well known, religious life is a term used to describe the various forms of life of those living in community under public vows of poverty, chastity, and obedience, following Church law and the rule and constitutions of their communities. This way of life, which has taken many forms and produced many saints and good works since the third century, is today in desperate condition in much of the world. Religious communities, which are required by their public commitment to follow their rule and constitutions, are dying out in many places, including America, Europe, and European-style countries such as Australia. The average age of most members of these religious communities today is well above sixty, while there are few or no recruits. Just a half century ago, in the years after World War II, religious life was flourishing, with thousands of new members each year and impressive works of charity and faith. The discipline of religious life at that time was somewhat oppressive and at times a bit inhuman. Members themselves were very sincere, with a high degree of dedication to God and the needs of the human race. Today, Catholic religious life is flourishing in Latin America, Asia, and Africa, while it appears to be dying in northern Europe and the English-speaking world.

What is much worse, it is not dying a holy death. Despite the presence of large numbers of older religious men and women who often yearn for the spirituality and obedience that they knew when they entered the life, some religious communities are filled with dissent from official Church teaching and even the norms of Sacred Scripture. Not only did religious garb, or the habit, disappear, but so did almost all vestiges of religious observance: daily community prayer, common life, personal poverty, a common apostolate, and even observance of the vow of chastity. This decline is simply amazing to me. I had profited greatly from being taught by Sisters of Saint Joseph, Sisters of Charity, and Dominican Sisters in both grammar school and high school. It seems that the loss of religious identity has been greater in communities of women than in orders of men. A possible reason is that many men religious still have the obligations of the priesthood, which provide a strong identity for them.

THEOLOGICAL CONFUSION

An honest analysis of the crisis would, I think, indicate the following causes:

First, there has been theological confusion and the acceptance of false teachings, which, although they might not be openly heretical, go against the tradition of the Church. These teachings include the notion that Christ was unsure of His identity or unaware of His mission. Writing about the need for reform a decade before the Second Vatican Council, the distinguished French Dominican Yves Congar indicated that any authentic reform must "begin with a return to the principles of Catholicism".[1] Cardinal Avery Dulles, using Father Congar's work as a starting

---

[1] Yves Congar, *True and False Reform in the Church*, cited in Avery Cardinal Dulles, "True and False Reform," in *First Things* (August/September 2003), p. 16.

point, presents his own excellent discussion of reform, including this comment:

> A genuinely Catholic reform will adhere to the fullness of Catholic doctrine, including not only the dogmatic definitions of popes and councils, but doctrines constantly and universally held as matters pertaining to the faith.[2]

Second, as Cardinal Dulles notes, there has been a jettisoning of much of Catholic tradition and identity; indeed, among the cargo sent over the side was the very tradition of religious life. He emphasizes, therefore, the traditions to which reforms must adhere:

> Any reform conducted in the Catholic spirit will respect the Church's styles of worship and pastoral life. It will be content to operate within the Church's spiritual and devotional heritage, with due regard for her Marian piety, her devotion to the saints, her high regard for the monastic life and the vows of religion, her penitential practices, and her Eucharistic worship.[3]

I may say very simply that—amid much denial and camouflage, hemming and hawing, about the signs of the times—most religious communities at present are fraternities or sororities of individual laypeople, who in varying ways struggle to observe the content of the vows they took long ago. Most are not unfaithful, but their communities are lost in the woods. Many have come to resemble secular institutes, yet often lack the focus and fidelity these possess. A small number of orders do preserve much of the discipline and identity of religious life, but so tentatively and apologetically that they fail to attract vocations because they are so obviously intimidated. The old proverb is relevant here: "If the trumpeter sounds an uncertain note, who will follow?"

A third reason for the decline of religious life, as well as for the general confusion in the Church, has its origins quite outside monasteries or convents. I refer here to the undermining of the credibility of the Scriptures, and especially of the Gospels. Sad to say, this undermining was done, at least among Catholics, by dedicated people whose goal,

---

[2] Dulles, p. 16.
[3] Ibid.

paradoxically, was to preserve the Scriptures' credibility. The complex story goes beyond the scope of this essay, and yet some indication is essential in order to see how religious life, traditionally seen as a Gospel-oriented life, lost its bearings. This loss was nowhere more obvious than in the many Franciscan communities, whose founder had said that his rule of life was simply to observe the Gospel.

In the last two centuries there has been much scholarly study of the historical origins of the sacred biblical texts, especially of the New Testament. Protestant scholars were followed by Catholic scholars, many of whom were involved in a tradition of study founded on agnosticism and skepticism. They tried to confront these anti-Christian interpretations, and they were in many ways successful. It must also be said that they tried to bring out truths and lessons helpful to the spiritual lives of their readers. Unfortunately, this scholarly and research-oriented approach was almost completely devoid of any understanding or application of the rules of scientific investigation.

The notion that a theory is a *tentatively* proposed solution to particular phenomena seems at times to have been completely lost. Theories were presented, and continue to be presented, as objective facts. Theories on the origin of the New Testament, some of which are very far from any observance of the discipline of scientific research, were given to seminarians, college students, religious education teachers, and even the faithful on Sunday morning. In most cases this has had a very negative effect. The now familiar opinions that Jesus did not do or say a particular thing, know or mean something else, or even understand what He was doing have undermined the foundations of religious life, as well as the faith of many educated Christians. Ironically, many of the same scholars held on to their own faith and took refuge in the Church's teaching and history. For instance, a number of them maintained that they could not prove the divinity of Christ, the Virgin Birth, or the Resurrection from the Scriptures, but they held on to these beliefs because of their membership in the Church and their conviction that the Christian message was true in general. This tactic was in itself a poorly camouflaged form of fideism, or intellectualized fundamentalism—the very thing they were trying to avoid. Msgr. Romano Guardini, an important Catholic theologian, along with a number of others, objected to the procedure of trying to define the historical Jesus as a figure contrasting with the Christ of faith.[4]

Having counseled clergy for decades, I can testify that many priests left the ministry because their faith had been undermined or at least had shifted from certitude to a hopeful supposition or positive opinion. In such an atmosphere, the personal experience of a relationship with Christ disappears. It stands to reason that a total commitment of one's life to discipleship, which is what religious life is supposed to be, was thereby undermined. So was the vocation of the diocesan priest. But because many religious orders provided security and retirement, some who had lost any sense of discipleship stayed on, most of them doing an honest day's work for their daily support, but with an ever diminishing sense of devotion and discipleship.

THE PSYCHOLOGIZING OF RELIGIOUS LIFE

The past fifty years have witnessed an unprecedented interest in popular psychology, and no group has been more psychologized than the clergy—first the Protestants, then the Catholics, and finally members of religious communities. Many schools of clinical psychology that were in vogue during that era—for example, the Freudian and the Jungian—have all but gone by the board for many of the same reasons that the historical/critical study of Scripture is beginning to be questioned. While claiming to be scientific, they repeatedly ignored the rules of scientific investigation.

Unfortunately, therapists of all kinds took on the work of spiritual directors and the care of souls, even if they were unbelievers. I have written about this popular procedure, which went against the tradition of religious life and substituted shaky psychological theories, some of them obviously antireligious, for guidance based on Scripture, tradition, and the teaching of the saints.[5] Psychology well understood and confined to its own proper provenance could be and was helpful, but psychology as a religion was a disaster.[6] The almost complete naturalism that followed thus lost sight of sin (both original and actual), grace, conversion, God's providence, and the necessity of faith, hope, and charity. There was no

---

[4] Romano Guardini, *The Lord*, trans. Elinor Castendyk Briefs (Chicago: Regnery, 1982).

[5] See Paul Vitz, *Psychology as Religion* (Grand Rapids, Mich.: Eerdmans, 1975).

[6] Ibid.

place for devotion to Christ, which was seen as a form of sublimation or a manifestation of the need to have a hero. The consequence was a series of scandals involving people identified as following the three vows but who actually followed none of them. It is one of the tragedies of the history of organized religion, including the Catholic Church, that when bad ideas enjoy a time of popular acceptance, little is done to identify and reject them, even when they do much harm. "[T]he sons of this world are wiser in their own generation than the sons of light" (Luke 16:8).

These are only some of the reasons why the bell of reform must begin to ring in the Church. Cardinal Dulles has summed up the situation well: "Religious illiteracy has sunk to a new low. We urgently need an effective program of catechesis and religious education on all levels. . . . Dissent is rampant. . . . Liturgical laws are often flouted. . . . Religious practice is falling off. . . . The immoral behavior of Catholics, both lay and clerical, is a cause of scandal and defections."[7]

An Answer to the Crisis

By 1987, a number of friars (including the first members of our renewal) had grown alarmed and disheartened at the current state of religious life. In this group, the two oldest friars, Father Andrew and I, had entered religious life in the days of very serious and earnest observance. Although it was a bit repressive and needed to be adjusted to the kind of men who were joining (many of them former servicemen), the life was undoubtedly authentic. It was a time when authority was exercised with a heavy hand, with little or no consulting of the members, causing mounting resentment. The renewal proposed by Pope John XXIII promised to bring about important changes, as did the various documents of Vatican II. Instead of renewal, however, a growing confusion in the 1970s and 1980s led to complete chaos. Personal prayer became platitudinous dialogue with God and Christ about what *we* wanted to do. A verse in the psalms seems so pertinent: "[I]f the foundations are destroyed,/ what can the righteous do?" (Psalm 11:3).[8]

---

[7] Dulles, 17–18.

[8] See books by Gerald A. Arbuckle, S.M.: *Strategies for Growth in Religious Life* (Alba House, 1987) and *Out of Chaos: Reforming Religious Congregations* (Paulist Press, 1988).

To their credit, most of the Capuchin provinces in Europe and America held out against the tide of decline for a long time. They were receiving vocations and had maintained a community life; but gradually they too succumbed to the forces that had already seriously disordered most other communities. All this decline happened despite the goodwill of many members, including many who were in charge. We must recall that confusion was everywhere and anomalies abounded. Embarrassing contradictions (such as "Sisters for Choice") became common, and allegedly Catholic colleges gave acceptance to all sorts of immoral and sacrilegious behavior on campuses. Slowly, despite a great deal of resistance, the same destructive elements that had already decimated other religious orders came to the Capuchins. A very small number of religious communities, currently thriving in the United States, managed to survive the tidal wave of confusion and disintegration.

One evening, an earnest young Capuchin priest warned me that vocations were being lost. "We must do something", he said. I heard a voice answer him, "Yes, we will do something." The voice was my own, but I had made no act of the will to say these words. I was so shocked by what I had said that I almost jumped up. Despite its troubles, I loved the community to which I belonged, and of course I still love the Capuchin ideal. A cold shudder ran through my body. I went to the chapel to pray. I felt both anxiety and relief. That visit to Christ in the Blessed Sacrament convinced me that I had a serious moral obligation to try to do something effective. I did not even think to raise the question, *Do others have a similar obligation?* I was only deeply aware of my own obligation. If I did not do something, I knew I would commit a mortal sin of negligence and omission, a lasting and habitual sin that could be forgiven only when I had fulfilled the obligation to try. It was clear to me that I was incapable of being a founder of anything. I did not have the ability, personality, gifts, or inspiration to begin a community. The next morning I called several friars, almost all of them young, whom I had known from the early days of their vocations. They had all voiced similar painful concerns regarding our order. It was then that the words came to my lips: "The axe is laid to the root of the trees."

In addition to Father Andrew Apostoli and me, the friars who came together were Fathers Glenn Sudano and Pio Mandato; and three friars who were in the seminary, Brothers Stanley Fortuna, Bob Lombardo, and Robert Stanion. This action required much courage of the student friars because it interrupted their seminary training; they ran the risk of never being ordained. Brother Joseph Nolan, a lay brother, was the eighth member of the group, and we were joined shortly by Brother John Lynch, a Capuchin in temporary vows (he is now a diocesan priest).

We made contact with twenty-one advisers—bishops, priests, and religious of some experience and importance in the Church and religious life. Twenty agreed that we should start a reform in the Capuchin tradition. In order to protect the seminarians (now all priests), we had initially to ask for leaves of absence in view of starting a new community. This was the only way they would be able to continue their studies.

It is an interesting point that there were and still are several communities of Capuchin friars in Europe and Latin America who chose to do the same thing. My hope always was that eventually we could be accepted as a community within the Capuchin Order. The Capuchins themselves had begun in just this way within the Franciscan Order; and at the time of the Reformation there were also Dominican and Augustinian reform communities existing within their parent orders.

"Why Did You Wait So Long?"

Finally the day came when I had to approach Cardinal O'Connor and ask him to sponsor our new community. I had known the cardinal for many years before he became a bishop, and we agreed on many topics. When I laid out our plans, tears ran down my face at the thought of leaving the Capuchins. The cardinal sat for a while in silence and then said, "I have one question. Why did you wait so long?"

He then directed me to notify the superior general in Rome and also the superiors of the New York and New Jersey provinces, from which we came. He also indicated that I could not leave the priests' retreat house where I was (and still am) working. This was a deep disappointment to me, for I wanted to live with the friars and work with the poor.

All this occurred before the popularity of the fax machine, so we wrote by air mail letter to the Capuchin Minister General, informing him of our plans. (I had written previously to the Father General, listing some serious problems I had observed.) Delivery of our letter was delayed, however, because of a postal strike in Italy; thus our provincial superiors learned of our decision before it could be communicated to the Capuchin General in Rome. Cardinal O'Connor took it upon himself to notify the papal nuncio and, through him, the Congregation of Religious.

Somehow rumors had begun to circulate, and the Capuchin provincial in New York was not surprised when we visited him in White Plains, New York. We asked permission to leave in a timely way. Several of us were delegates to the provincial chapter in New York, and we resigned immediately from the chapter.

On April 28, 1987, we received permission from the Capuchin provincials to leave, and we began our community with very few resources but with many friends. Father John Corriveau, then general councilor of the English-speaking Capuchins and now the minister general, soon after came to New York. He treated us kindly and with understanding, although he clearly did not approve of our decision. Considering the disappointment and upset that our decision caused to many Capuchins, I must say that we were treated very well and with fraternal kindness by almost all our confreres.

Renewal Comes to the Bronx

In the 1980s, the New York archdiocese had begun to close redundant national parishes, and a former Polish parish, Saint Adalbert's in the Bronx, was offered to us as our home. It was located in an area known then as Fort Apache, one of the city's worst sections. Today this property, which still belongs to the diocese, houses two friaries—Saint Crispin's and Our Lady of Angels—and a night shelter. The former parish school is home to our youth program and Hope Line, a Catholic-sponsored social agency. Next to the friaries, the impressive Saint Anthony's Residence for homeless men stands in what was once a burned-out building. The wonderful gift from Divine Providence of Saint Adalbert's parish came when we had no other place to go.

We dedicated our first friary to a Capuchin lay brother, Saint Crispin of Viterbo, who was famous for writing scathing letters to members of the clergy needing reform. He was the first saint canonized by Pope John

Paul II. We chose this crusty old brother as our patron for two reasons: to honor the Pope and to indicate that we had no other goal than to be loyal to the ideal of the traditional Capuchin piety.

A few blocks from Saint Crispin's is the first convent of the Missionaries of Charity founded in the United States. After our visit to the Capuchin provincial, I went to visit Mother Teresa, who was then staying at the convent. She was most encouraging, although this was the first she had heard of our plans. When I told her that we had $800 and eight men, she said, "Don't worry. God has lots of money." Although we now spend almost $2 million a year on our work with the poor, we have never run out of funds needed to do this work.

Mother Teresa also pointedly emphasized two things for our consideration: first, we must follow the Gospel and lead the life of the first followers of Jesus. She reminded us that He was with us always in the Blessed Sacrament, and she encouraged us to make a daily Eucharistic holy hour part of our community schedule, something we have faithfully done. She also emphasized the importance of identifying what we believed God wanted us to do and remaining faithful to that decision. We told her that in imitation of the early Capuchins, we wanted to work with the very poor, provide shelter for the homeless, and do evangelical preaching to young and old alike. Thanks be to God, that is what we have done.

The Congregation of Religious required that we spend the next three years on a leave of absence from the Capuchin Order, and we had no canonical identity. No further steps could be taken. With the help of many friends we began that day to live the traditional Capuchin life and to prepare to take care of homeless men. From the first day at Saint Crispin's we offered the community Mass and recited the liturgy of the hours. Evening prayer forms part of our Eucharistic holy hour. That holy hour, our legacy from Mother Teresa, is the most precious gift we have received. It has held us together through thick and thin. Because of our small numbers in the early years, the Dominican nuns of Corpus Christi monastery, located near us, in Hunts Point, invited us to celebrate the solemn liturgies of Christmas and Holy Week with them.

Cardinal O'Connor and the Capuchin superiors informed me that they would deal with me as if I were the superior. I had no authority other than what the friars chose to give me, but that was quite enough. Although I was to remain at Trinity Retreat, to which I had been assigned some years before by Cardinal Cooke, Father Andrew received permission to leave the retreat house, where he had been associate director, and live with the friars and work as the director of formation. His place at Trinity Retreat was taken by Father Eugene Fulton, a priest of the Byzantine Eastern rite, who has become an affiliate of our community and the very competent spiritual director of many of our friars as well as many diocesan priests. We had to send back our Capuchin habits, so we adopted the same habit but in gray, which was the original color of Franciscan and Capuchin habits. A number of new Franciscan reform communities have also adopted gray for their habits.

And so we began.

A New Way of Life

In the 1970s and 1980s, the South Bronx was in terrible condition. Mother Teresa told me it was the worst thing she had ever seen. Empty burned-out buildings occupied block after block, and the streets were filled with broken glass and wrecked cars. There was no law and order. Drugs were sold openly in the street, and gun battles could be heard almost every night. There was only one occupied apartment house on our street, and the people who lived there clung to the friars for safety.

In this arena of almost complete social disintegration we began to care for the poor, especially poor children of the neighborhood. We struck up a fine relationship with the local firehouse, and to this day we share a parking lot. It was with great joy and thanks to God that we opened the Padre Pio Shelter in the old Saint Adalbert's convent on December 23 of that year. Every night since then, except for a two-week period when the friars went on pilgrimage to Rome, the shelter has welcomed eighteen men from the receiving center for the homeless at Saint Agnes Church in Manhattan. Since we wanted to work with the poor, our Lord had put us in exactly the right place. During the summer of 1987 we also began preparing our provisional constitutions, which were based on the older constitutions of the Capuchin Order but also borrowed from the newer ones.

We were soon joined by a small group of young women who had been discussing religious life with Father Andrew. One of them was Lucille Cutrone, who is now Sister Lucille, the Community Servant of the Franciscan Sisters of the Renewal. For a time the sisters were in the care of Sister Theresa and Sister Joan May, who had come from another Franciscan community.

VOCATIONS COME

One of the very surprising things in the very early days was the number of people who wanted to join our community. Unfortunately, we were unable to receive any candidates, because we had no canonical existence and we were only religious on leaves of absence. However, a few months after our establishment, Cardinal O'Connor permitted us to receive some quasi-candidates, who began formation under the direction of Father Andrew with the assistance of Father Glenn. Of several fine men who tried, two persevered. They are now Father Herald Brock and Brother Michael Kmiotek, the first professed members of our community. In the meantime our three seminarians began studies at Saint Joseph's Seminary, Dunwoodie, where Father Andrew and I had taught for many years. This fine seminary, known for its loyal teaching of Catholic doctrine, has provided a solid foundation for my life for three decades of teaching. I had been fired from several other seminaries for being too Catholic. (Of course, that was not the stated reason; those in charge did not need a reason to fire a part-time professor.) Therefore, I can only say thank God for Dunwoodie, where our friars now are a significant percentage of the student body.

By the summer of 1988, our formation program had taken shape. There were four quasi-candidates for the friars, and the sisters began with six laywomen at the same time. The friar candidates moved with Father Glenn to the vacant convent of Sacred Heart parish in the Highbridge section of the Bronx. It was a period of spartan living and poverty, which we remember as a happy time, when we were really pilgrims and strangers in this world.

In August, with Father Andrew as their guide, the two sisters and six candidates for the sisters' community moved into the old Saint Adalbert's convent, occupying the floors above the shelter. This was not an easy situation for them, but there were no complaints. Having a recognized status in the Church as a private association of the faithful, our sisters were free to admit candidates and move ahead with formation. It amuses me to call our formation program precisely by that name. The term *formation program* was popular in the 1960s and 1970s, and the word *program* is often used for unnecessarily complicated things. Our formation was not unnecessarily complicated.

Although the brothers and sisters lived in the inner city, surrounded by violence and all of the problems that New York knew at that time, our formation stressed silence and prayer. You can be silent and prayerful on the subway if you make up your mind to do so. We never felt the need to move to a quiet country setting and start a formation program in some beautiful valley. Our formation houses were poor, plain, and simple. The brothers kept up a challenging prayer schedule, along with fasting and other things that are part of religious formation. They attended a number of classes and were taken to the countryside from time to time for quiet retreats.

Our community continued to work hard caring for the poor and maintaining the buildings the archdiocese had lent us. The group in formation was advancing; and by 1989, Cardinal O'Connor permitted three of our candidates to become quasi-novices. Father Andrew was named novice master, assisted by Father Glenn, and they moved into the top floor of the Augustinian parish rectory of Saint Rita.

PILGRIMAGE TO ITALY

In October of 1988, the entire group of friars, sisters, and candidates went to Rome and Assisi as guests of Edward Walley (who later became a priest). We wanted to appreciate Saint Francis and his followers better—and also obtain a papal blessing on our endeavors. We were guests of the Don Guanella Fathers in Rome; they are an institute that cares for the mentally retarded. With the help of Father Philip Blaine, a Conventual Franciscan, we were given the use of an ancient friary at Rocca San Angelo, outside Assisi. This building has an incredibly beautiful chapel, on the ceiling of which are Cimabue's original sketches of his paintings in the great basilica of Saint Francis. We were fascinated by all of Assisi, and drawn especially to the tiny friary called the *Carcere* (because it was once

OCTOBER 1988: *Community pilgrimage to Rome.*

the jail) and the little cells in the woods, where the original friars prayed in solitude.

While in Rome, the friars of our community also had a formal visit with Jerome Cardinal Hamer, O.P., then prefect of the Congregation of Religious. He was scheduled to meet with us for a half hour before lunch, but he stayed on for almost two hours—an intrusion into the midday meal that is almost unheard of in Rome. The cardinal was most kind and encouraging, but he suggested we try to work out some arrangement that would permit us to remain under the jurisdiction of the Capuchin General. He gave the example of a group of young Dominican friars who five centuries before had done as we did. Known as the Dominican Congregation of San Marco in Florence, they were a reform community that included Saint Antoninus, who became archbishop of Florence, and the great artist Blessed (Fra) Angelico. I asked the cardinal: Who had been their leader? He cleared his throat and said quietly, "Savonarola." Knowing that there were several people who might like to burn me at the stake, I was not encouraged by this revelation. (Two years later, we tried to work out an arrangement like that of the friars of San Marco, but, as I will relate, we did not succeed.)

Ten years later, I was in Assisi again, and looked one day over the valley of Spoleto. I felt a sense of peace. Even though I was still a very mediocre person, I was surrounded by young sisters and friars who were trying to discern how they could do more in their Franciscan life, not how they could do less. When I had attended the general chapter of the Capuchins held in Rome back in 1970, I had felt uncomfortable when we visited Assisi. The thought of my own mediocrity and failure to achieve the ideals of Saint Francis had made me discouraged and ashamed. Visiting the same place in 1988 with this energetic, dedicated group of young people, I felt very relieved. We also offered Mass at the convent where Saint Clare is buried. I came away with the impression that this holy and gentle woman was praying for us and would remain our close friend.

We had the wonderful experience of grasping the hand of Pope John Paul II and asking for his blessing at a general audience. Divine Providence put us in the front row, enabling us to greet this great pope personally, whose teaching and life are the guiding stars of our community. We also gathered for a picture and prayer at the base of the huge granite obelisk in the center of Saint Peter's Square. In 1586, Pope Sixtus V had transferred it from Nero's circus and placed it in the square as a monument to Rome's early martyrs. Around the base of the obelisk the blood of hundreds, perhaps thousands, of Roman Christians had been shed in terrible torment for the amusement of the pagan world. The words inscribed on the base of the obelisk had particular meaning for our little band of twenty or so fervent sisters and brothers: "Christ conquers, Christ captains, Christ commands. Christ defends His people from every evil." The Latin words sound less military than the English: *Christus vincit, Christus regnat, Christus imperat. Christus ab omni malo plebem suam defendat.* This inscription gave us great encouragement. Despite all the skepticism about Christ, even about His intention in offering His life as a sacrifice of obedience to take away the world's sins, despite all the erosion of personal devotion to our Savior, I believe that our little group, so small in proportion to Saint Peter's Square, infinitesimal in relation to the Church and the world, was filled with the conviction that He was with us because we chose to be with Him.

During our few days in Rome, we were delighted to attend the impressive beatification ceremony for a saintly and heroic Capuchin priest, Blessed Honorat Kosminski. He had saved the Capuchin Order in Poland from extinction during the Russian occupation before World War I. He had also been founder or co-founder of no fewer than fourteen congregations of sisters, including the Felician Sisters, who befriended us with food and encouragement in our early days. We returned home, grateful to God for the blessings of our pilgrimage.

New Influences: Pro-Life

By early 1989, about two years after our beginning, some powerful directions began to develop in the community. As I look back, I think they were unfolding gradually in the hearts of the first members under the guidance of the Holy Spirit. These directions have defined our life and work to this day, and I hope they will continue to lead us in the future.

The first of these was the pro-life movement. To those who would listen to her, Mother Teresa often stated: "Any nation that kills its children cannot survive." When asked what she thought about abortion, she often responded: "What do you think that Jesus thinks about abortion?" The Holy Father had called for strong public action against abortion in *Evangelium Vitae*.

> In view of laws which permit abortion and in view of efforts, which here and there have been successful, to legalize euthanasia, movements and initiatives to raise social awareness in defense of life have sprung up in many parts of the world. When, in accordance with their principles, such movements act resolutely but without resorting to violence, they promote a wider and more profound consciousness of the value of life, and evoke and bring about a more determined commitment to its defense.[9]

---

[9] Pope John Paul II, *Evangelium Vitae* (1995), 27.1.

Father Benedict (right) and Father Fidelis with the late Bishop George Lynch (standing), waiting to be taken to the police station after having been arrested for saying the Rosary in front of an abortuary in Dobbs Ferry, New York.

Everyone has an obligation to be at the service of life. This is a properly "ecclesial" responsibility, which requires concerted and generous action by all the members and by all sectors of the Christian community. This community commitment does not, however, eliminate or lessen the responsibility of each individual, called by the Lord to "become the neighbor" of everyone: "Go and do likewise" (Luke 10:37).

Together we all sense our duty to preach the Gospel of life, to celebrate it in the liturgy and in our whole existence, and to serve it with the various programs and structures which support and promote life.[10]

---

[10] Ibid., 79.3, 4.

A unique responsibility belongs to health-care personnel: doctors, pharmacists, nurses, chaplains, men and women Religious, administrators, and volunteers. Their profession calls them to be guardians and servants of human life. . . .

Volunteer workers have a specific role to play: they make a valuable contribution to the service of life when they combine professional ability and generous, selfless love. The Gospel of life inspires them to lift their feelings of goodwill toward others to the heights of Christ's charity; to renew every day, amid hard work and weariness, their awareness of the dignity of every person; to search out people's needs and, when necessary, to set out on new paths where needs are greater but care and support weaker.[11]

The friars and sisters took the teachings of the encyclical very seriously. Many of us had been involved in the pro-life movement long before we started our community. It was only logical, therefore, that the pro-life apostolate should become very much a focal point of our community's work. We joined the brave and dedicated souls who pray and counsel in front of abortuaries. Particularly on Saturday mornings everyone who is not fulfilling some other apostolic responsibility is expected to be praying in front of an abortuary. Many of our friars and sisters have been involved in pro-life rescues. Over the years we have made enough of an impact that some pro-abortion groups have attacked us on the Internet. As a result of our pro-life work, two of our community, Father Fidelis Moscinski and I, did some time in prison, along with Bishop George Lynch, a great priest, a witness against abortion, and a champion of the sanctity of all human life. Before he joined our community, Father Conrad Osterhout spent a month in jail in Buffalo, New York, and a year in the Lehigh County Jail, in Bethlehem, Pennsylvania, for his pro-life activities.

Of course, it is not enough to give witness to a young mother who is considering abortion, so that she will change her mind and save the life of her child. We have to help this poor mother. The friars became involved

---

[11] Ibid., 89.2; 90.1.

with service to poor expectant mothers, referring them to a safe haven or shelter. Since the beginning of our community we have supported the Good Counsel Homes, founded by Chris Bell, which since 1987 have provided a safe and comfortable home for homeless and needy mothers and their babies. Good Counsel may provide for a mother for up to two years, helping her make a new start and become self-sufficient.

Our community has also helped the Sisters of Life, who were founded by Cardinal O'Connor to assist in all issues related to the preservation of human life, particularly the care of mothers and children who have no resources and who need a loving home. The Sisters of Life also follow a traditional religious life and have grown as the friars have done.

NEW WORK FOR THE POOR

The friars began to receive financial support for their work with the poor. These funds have been kept entirely separate from the alms we collect for our living expenses (which are small), health and building insurance expenses (which are high), and the cost of educating our seminarians. As the support for our work with the poor grew, so did the work, including a large regular food distribution to certified needy families, especially elderly people on public assistance who receive nothing other than social security or welfare. Single mothers and their children are also our special concern. But good Christians should try to tithe, to give a regular part of their income for the works of charity. For this reason we started, early on, to help other hands-on good works, such as other shelters run by volunteers or expectant-mother care centers. We also try to help with Catholic school tuition for children of very poor families who can profit by the discipline and educational opportunities of parochial schools and who may need the protection that such schools can give in the midst of the slums.

THE LIFE OF PRAYER

Another powerful influence on our community was the recognition of the need for more prayer and solitude. The community rule requires that each week one day be set aside for prayer and silence in the friaries and convents and that once a month each member go apart and spend two days in solitude and silence. This is not easily done in the midst of the city, so the Lord provided us with the Shenck farm in upstate New York. The

Shenck family no longer used the farm for vacations, but they still had affectionate memories for it and for their uncle, an old Slovak priest, who had given it to them. For years the 140-year-old farmhouse and two little hermitages the friars built nearby have offered a wonderful quiet retreat to be "alone with the Alone"—*solus cum solo*. Later, a friend of the community, Rita Woodford, donated a large tract of land in the Catskill Mountains, where the friars built a large hermitage, with a few cells scattered in the woods. Saint Francis Hermitage and the smaller Saint Clare Hermitage, purchased by Cathy Hickey for the sisters, have provided a wonderful place for solitude and contemplation.

WORK WITH YOUTHS

A further significant influence that came into our lives was work with poor children and teenagers. Even in the worst days of Fort Apache in the Bronx, many youngsters still lived there in the ruins. Their only playground was the dangerous street strewn with debris, where drugs were sold in the open, where wilding gangs of teenagers terrified people, and where gun battles often killed innocent passers-by. Thank God, law and order gradually returned to the city. The beleaguered police officers in our precinct discontinued the nickname Fort Apache and (ironically) chose as their new name for the precinct station—the Little House on the Prairie.

The young friars and sisters enthusiastically took on work with area youths. Generous friends helped to transform the auditorium of our parish school into a very good gym. All sorts of religious, educational, and recreational activities take place in what is now called the Saint Francis Youth Center. The number of people for whom the friars and sisters care has grown so large over time that they are almost engulfed by people—except, that is, in the sanctuary of the friary and convent. The young come for activities and education, the elderly come for assistance and encouragement, and lots of people in between, especially poor mothers, who come because they desperately need help. As our work grew, a number of volunteers came along to help. Father Bob Lombardo organized the dedicated group of Lay Associates, who have the opportunity to help the poor by sorting clothes and donations, assisting with food preparation, and bringing direct services to the poor.

By the spring of 1990, our burgeoning community welcomed a new candidate, Brother Terry Messer, a professed Franciscan friar of the Lithuanian American custody. We still had no official status in canon law, but that was about to come to an end. On April 2, in the Church of Saint John the Evangelist in Manhattan, Cardinal O'Connor celebrated a Mass that marked our official existence as a religious association in the Church. He was assisted by the Vicar General, Bishop Patrick Sheridan, and our faithful friend Bishop William McCormack. The ceremony of our establishment took place quietly but with great joy. In the sacristy before Mass, we signed the documents of our dispensation from vows as Capuchins. After the reading of the Gospel, the decree of our establishment as a public association of the faithful was read by Bishop Sheridan. We then proceeded to take again the same vows we had been living under: poverty, chastity, and obedience. The new vows had a slightly different wording to accommodate the name of our new community.

We had no intention of being anything other than Capuchins and had asked to be allowed to use that designation. Permission to do so was refused, however, even though other communities of friars and nuns who are called Capuchin are not under the jurisdiction of the order itself. Father Andrew and I were particularly saddened to leave the Capuchins, to which we had belonged for a combined total of almost seventy years. I was gratefully consoled by the presence of the New York Capuchin provincial, Father John Rathschmidt, who was kind enough to concelebrate the Mass with us. A Capuchin archbishop from another country wrote consolingly to me that these were mere pieces of paper and that I would always be a Capuchin. That was all I wanted. After the ceremony, we all made a little pilgrimage to upper Manhattan to pray at the tomb of Saint Frances Xavier Cabrini, the only saint whose remains are in New York. This intrepid and dedicated servant of the poor and the immigrants seemed to be a good patron for our little group, which worked in the same boroughs where she had brought the light of the Gospel and the loving care of Christ.

A little later we packed up the old vans we had collected (we don't buy cars but use those given to us), and we all went, sisters and friars, to

Montreal to visit the Oratory of Saint Joseph and the tomb of Blessed André Bessette, the humble lay brother who had built the great shrine. We also went to pray at the tomb of Blessed Kateri Tekakwitha, the Mohawk girl who brought a sense of holiness and mysticism to early Native American converts to the Church. The tears ran down our faces as we prayed at the tombs of these humble souls who proved that the Lord has filled the hungry with good things and has lifted up the lowly.

THE LORD WAS WITH US

As we drove across the long Champlain bridge into Montreal, the bolts on the steering mechanism of the first van in our five-car cortege broke, making it impossible to steer. The driver was able to stop the van at the end of the steep descent of the bridge; but the muffler in the van following behind it exploded like a bomb, frightening motorists and friars alike. Both vans had to be pushed from the bridge entrance. A man on the sidewalk pointed out an auto-repair garage half a block away. The Armenian owners were astonished by our arrival but were most helpful. It was four o'clock on a Friday afternoon, and they explained that it would be difficult to get parts before Monday. They promised to try. By five o'clock, as if by a miracle of Divine Providence, we drove both vans away to the modest Foyer des Pèlerins at Saint Joseph's Oratory, where we stayed for two days. The mechanics reluctantly charged us $100 Canadian for the extensive repairs.

While we were in Montreal, where religious garb has all but disappeared in a tide of antireligion, several people asked us if we belonged to the Frères de l'Emmanuel. We were told that they dressed exactly as we do, with a gray robe and a hemp rope.

So we went to visit their little friary, and it was like meeting relatives we never knew we had. Eventually Brothers Denis and François of the Frères came to stay with us in New York and received some formation, as neither had been a religious before his efforts to become Franciscan. They returned to Canada and are now doing very well ministering in the poorest section of Montreal; the Frères also have an outreach to Africa.

After the establishment of our community as a public association of the faithful, we had an existence in canon law, and things began to move fast. Brothers Bob Lombardo and Stanley Fortuna were ordained deacons in May by Bishop Sean O'Malley, O.F.M. Cap., the Ordinary of Fall River, Massachusetts, at Saint Adalbert's Church. Shortly thereafter, Brother Bob was ordained a priest. A chapter was held, and I was elected to a second three-year term as community servant, with Fathers Andrew and Glenn as councilors.

That summer we moved the Padre Pio Shelter to the unused basement of Saint Adalbert's school, which was renovated to provide a haven for the homeless. Work also began on Saint Anthony's Residence, a vacant building next to Saint Crispin's Friary, to provide housing for homeless men.

Our formal establishment also made possible the profession of first vows by Brothers Michael and Herald; and our formation program moved to Saint Felix Friary in Yonkers, New York, the former convent of Most Holy Trinity parish. The friary is located in a beautiful little square with three churches dedicated to the most holy Trinity: along with the Catholic Church, Russian Orthodox and Lutheran churches adjoin the square. Father Andrew was appointed novice master.

Among the postulants received in September 1990 was Richard Roemer, who had originally studied with the Capuchins in Wisconsin and who has become vicar of our community. Brother Herald and Brother Terry joined Brother Robert Stanion as students at Dunwoodie, and Brother Michael became part of the staff of Saint Crispin's. On the feast of the Immaculate Conception, Brother Stanley was ordained to the priesthood by Auxiliary Bishop William McCormick at Saint Adalbert's Church. His ordination brought the year to a beautiful close and was an event of great joy for the community. It was now clear that we were becoming part of the Church's ongoing life.

The next year and a half was a time of consolidation. Following his profession in January 1992, Brother Richard began the Saint Francis Youth Center program in the old school. This has steadily developed over the years, and he later initiated the Summer Life program, a spiritually based day-camp. Father Robert was ordained a priest on May 16 at Saint Patrick's Cathedral; and in September, along with two others, Brother Fidelis began his formation.

About this time, our work of evangelizing youths suddenly began to take shape. The first "Youth 2000" retreat was held in Texas that August. Ann Brawley, along with other laypeople, had established this program to attract young people to a Eucharistic weekend retreat, and it was a very powerful experience for them. The movement began to spread around the country; and the following year, the first meeting was held in New York. It was a great success, and from then on the name of the Franciscan Friars and Sisters of the Renewal was associated in people's minds with this remarkable spiritual movement. Young people who have little or no knowledge of devotion to the Holy Eucharist come for the weekend and participate in Mass, adoration, processions, individual confession, music, lectures, and sermons. Most of those who attend the weekend go home quite changed.

The New York Youth 2000 office is now established at Saint Francis House in Brooklyn. The latter is a residence for homeless boys, which I began in 1967; the directorship has been taken over by Joseph Campo, who also runs Youth 2000 in New York. Mr. Campo is also director of the Grassroots Renewal Project, a lay-operated evangelical effort, which produces audio- and videotapes, and which owes its existence to the dedication of Father Glenn.

DAYS OF BLESSINGS

The friars enjoyed an especially beautiful year in 1993. Many things that began that year have defined the development of our community.

On June 13, Saint Anthony's Residence was dedicated. It provides a private room, as well as a dining room and common areas, for sixty-five men, some of whom are able to support themselves with modest jobs, while others are elderly, ill, or incapacitated and receive public assistance. Father Bob Lombardo was responsible for the entire reconstruction of the burned-out wreck of a building, which is now a very handsome one indeed. He was also director for the first eleven years of the residence, which has a fine reputation and has become the flagship of similar residences for the homeless in New York City.

Father Bob also supervised the renovation of Saint Adalbert's Church, which was then a hundred years old, making it now one of the most beautiful churches in the Bronx, and he likewise oversaw the renovation of the Padre Pio Shelter.

That summer, our general chapter elected Father Andrew as community servant and Father Robert Stanion as vicar. Having already served two three-year terms, I decided that the community should follow the Capuchin custom of a maximum of two terms in office.

In July, Brothers Michael, Herald, and Terry made their final vows, an important event that symbolized the permanence of the community. Almost all the friars and sisters went to World Youth Day in Denver in August 1993. We took with us a number of young people, including one young woman who later joined the sisters' community. The visit of Pope John Paul II to that event was both edifying and triumphal. The local diocese asked us to make use of a church that was without a priest at the time because the rectory was being rebuilt. In the midst of the renovation, among the plaster boards and buckets of nails, we camped out in the rectory and were delighted to do so. Thousands of young people marched past our door on their way to the stadium. It was a wonderful opportunity to meet people and introduce them to our new religious community.

By September 1993, it became obvious that with our growing number of vocations we needed more room. The archdiocese arranged to give us the use of the convent of Saint Ann's Church, on Bainbridge Avenue in the Bronx. Father Glenn directed it as a house for postulants. We also had a very good class of novices that year, including Brothers Bernard Murphy, Thomas Cacciola, and Angelus Houle, who were subsequently ordained priests for our community.

In the spring of 1994, the community was again blessed by the ordination of Fathers Herald and Terry. Among the postulants joining us that fall was Brother Shawn O'Connor. In December we were pleased to receive into our community a priest of the Third Order Regular. When he entered our community, Father John Osterhout, who had been dean at Franciscan University in Steubenville, Ohio, took the name of Saint Conrad, a nineteenth-century Capuchin lay brother. Franciscan University has made the spiritual life of its students a top priority, along with academic excellence. A large number of those who have applied for admission to our communities of friars and sisters have been graduates of Franciscan University, and many others have visited.

Things seemed to be going well, but there were storm clouds on the horizon.

STORM CLOUDS

As often happens in new religious communities, especially Franciscan communities, there were disagreements about the apostolate and the observance of the Rule of Saint Francis. Anyone who has read the saint's life knows that almost no one can live up to his example. It is very similar with the Gospel. All sincere Christians and Franciscans try to do the best they can with their own personal limitations and those of their times.

At various times in history, people have tried to emphasize this or that aspect of Saint Francis's life, particularly the radical observance of poverty. Although untold numbers have tried, it does seem that the only person to succeed in a perfect imitation of Saint Francis was his contemporary Saint Clare. Many Franciscan saints have lived in solid buildings, where bells rang, meals were served on time, and the observance of religious life devoutly fulfilled. Some reform-minded Franciscans have even lived painfully in institutionalized communities that were not very inspired by Saint Francis's example.

Towards the end of 1994, Father Pio, Brother Joseph Nolan, and four friars in temporary vows announced that they were leaving to form a new Franciscan community. They would call themselves the Franciscans of the Primitive Observance and would be under the jurisdiction of Bishop O'Malley of Fall River. At the same time Sister Theresa May led six sisters, most of them in novitiate, from the community for the same reason. It was a dark and anxious time for us.

Unfortunately, the community's apostolate had become a bone of contention, and the building of Saint Anthony's Residence was especially a subject of disagreement. Everyone agreed, however, that prayer, contemplation, and occasional withdrawal from the world were indispensable to our attempt to live the Capuchin ideal.

The Franciscans of the Primitive Observance were seeking a very strict material poverty and a life of preaching. To this day, they have no vehicles, telephones, or refrigeration. As with all zealous reform movements, after the initial fervor come some accommodations for survival that had not been foreseen. Over the years, feelings between the two communities of friars have become more pleasant and fraternal, and the Franciscans of the Primitive Observance have grown slowly but steadily. Members of both communities sometimes meet at pro-life activities, and there is the occasional visit back and forth.

When Cardinal O'Connor preached at the ceremony at which our community became an association of the faithful, he mentioned that it was common for Franciscan communities to give rise to other Franciscan communities, adding that he would not be surprised if that were to happen with our community. He seemed to show an ability to predict the future.

Bishop O'Malley was caught in a painful dilemma. The brothers who left us had confided their plans in him. He was a close friend also of our community, but because of the element of confidentiality he was unable to tell us what was happening. Now, as Archbishop of Boston, he has remained on good terms with both communities over the years.

The disagreements among the friars and sisters during this period made for a most painful time, especially for those in charge, notably Father Andrew. Fortunately, Sister Lucille Cutrone was one of those who remained with the Franciscans Sisters of the Renewal. She eventually became superior and has held that office ever since. As of this writing, the Sisters are showing encouraging signs of growth, and new candidates are coming every year.

In order to survive this challenge, the friars sought the help of Father Joseph Fitzpatrick, S.J., a faculty member at Fordham University. Father Fitzpatrick worked with the Puerto Rican and Hispanic community for decades and brought to that field his sociological knowledge and resources. He had the honorary title "Puerto Rican of the Year" in New York. He was extremely kind in serving as a facilitator for us and helping us through this difficult period. The same is true of Sister Catherine Quinn, P.B.V.M., who was vicar for religious at the time and stood by us throughout.

Another part of our response to this challenge was to call an extraordinary chapter early in 1995, when we began a formal study, called the

Capuchin Identity Study, to determine from Capuchin history the precise intention of the early members of our order. The study turned out to be quite beneficial and led to some surprising insights. After considering the example of the lives of the early Capuchins, from around 1535, we discovered that many of them worked in hospitals. In those days, a hospital was not an agency that specialized in advanced medical care but rather a shelter for the poor and homeless and particularly for the sick who had no one to care for them. The first Capuchin church in Rome, Our Lady of Miracles, had a hospital attached to it. In 1545, the Capuchins took over the largest charity hospital in the world, the Pammatone in Genoa, which continued its good work until destroyed by American bombs in 1944. Without even trying to do so, we had followed the example of the early Capuchins, doing what they had done.

From their founding until the late nineteenth century, Capuchins engaged in hospital work with the sick, often with plague and epidemic victims. Some provinces lost as many as half or two thirds of their members to the diseases of those for whom they cared. Saint Francis Mary Camporosso (1804–1866) worked among plague victims in the port of Genoa and died as a result of the same disease.

There were also a number of blessings and positive developments in 1995. Brother Richard made his final vows, as did Sister Lucille, the pioneer of the sisters' community. In September, six postulants were received, including Brothers Francis Edkins (our first English vocation), Leo Joseph Fisher (Texas), Ephrem Maria Ali (Trinidad), and Martin de Porres Ervin (Nebraska).

In 1996, Father Andrew was elected to a second term as community servant, and the Capuchin Identity Study was presented at the June chapter. Despite the departure of six friars, we were again experiencing growing pains. The archdiocese gave us the use of an old retreat house in the middle of Harlem, which became Saint Joseph's Friary, our novitiate for several years. Those familiar with the city will know that 142nd Street and Broadway is one of the pulsing centers of life in Harlem. Half a block from this corner was a retreat house that had been used more recently by the Cursillo Movement. The friars, directed by Brother Michael, did a great deal of work to renovate the building. In September of that year, seventeen postulants, our largest class, entered the community, and they were able to move into the Harlem friary a few months later with Father Glenn as the novice master.

The opening of Saint Joseph's Friary with such a large class was a tremendous boon for us from Divine Providence. That we were also able to pay for the building's repairs was itself almost miraculous. The archdiocese had promised to give us $50,000, and we were to raise an equal sum for the cost of repair. However, once the renovation was under way, we discovered such interesting and disconcerting things as the fact that the electrical service and wiring had been installed by the Edison Company, as one of the first buildings in the area to receive electric lights. The insulating fabric around the wiring crumbled to the touch, and the whole building had to be rewired.

All in all, the cost of repairs came to double the original estimate, and the friars did not have sufficient money. In the midst of this financial worry, a gentleman phoned one day and asked if he could discuss his spiritual life. He came to see me, arriving from Wall Street in a hired limousine. We talked on, well into the night, and then he said he would be going home on the subway. I protested that it would be a long and dangerous trip, and suggested instead that he stay the night. He agreed, and slept in a sleeping bag on the friary floor, as the friars do. As he was leaving the next morning, he handed me a check. I had not spoken to him at all of our financial difficulties. After he left, I looked at the check, which I thought at first was for $1,000. When I looked again, I saw it was for $10,000. I looked a third time and saw, finally, that it was actually for $100,000—exactly the amount of money needed to finish the repairs at Saint Joseph's. At present, Saint Joseph's Friary is our house for postulants.

In 1997, we consolidated our growth after the shock of the departure of six of the brethren. Brothers Fidelis and Bernard professed final vows, and in September, Mother Teresa, a dear friend to our community, died in India. This was an extremely moving event, as most people will remember. Mother Teresa had stood beside our community during the previous ten years. She had often not been well during that time; but whenever she came to New York, we made a point of visiting her, and she was always extremely interested in how we were doing. The friars also attempted to assist Mother Teresa with the needs of her sisters, particularly with the foundation of the contemplative Missionaries of Charity.

The sisters phoned Father Andrew and me one day just before Mother Teresa was to return to India (it was eight weeks before her death), and invited us to offer Mass for her. It was an immense privilege. At that point, Mother Teresa could not stand, but lay on a mobile bed in the corner of the chapel. She seemed to be filled with joy and happiness as she told us of the amazing growth of her community. I remember her saying, "We now have five hundred and twenty-five tabernacles." That was how she referred to each of the sisters' convents.

Since her death we have learned that Mother Teresa lived a life of great spiritual darkness. She lived through what religious writers call the dark night of the soul for many years, although it was not evident from her cheerful disposition. It is frightening to read of her spiritual darkness, which she reveals in letters to her spiritual director. Nonetheless, there was always a smile—that was Mother's great secret.

It is my impression that by the time we said Mass for her that day, less than two months before her death, the darkness was over. She could already see the gates of eternal life. As we left the convent that day, I said to Father Andrew that we would not see her again. She was going home to eternal life.

CANONICAL RELIGIOUS—AGAIN

At this juncture in the life of our community we experienced more growing pains. We needed a place for our seminarians to live within walking distance of Saint Joseph's Seminary in Yonkers. By an act of Divine Providence, we obtained the use of the convent of Saint Casimir's parish, in a declining neighborhood about a mile from the seminary. Today it houses a number of friars, who are within easy reach of the seminary. It opened as our student house, with Brother Michael as the servant and Father Herald as the vicar.

In 1998, the largest group of friars made first vows, and Brothers Angelus Houle and Thomas Cacciola professed their final vows. That year also Fathers Richard and Bernard were ordained to the priesthood.

We were still not a full-fledged religious community. This took a bit of work and letter writing and the complete support of Cardinal

MAY 1999: *With Cardinal O'Connor at St. Patrick's Cathedral on the day of the formal establishment of our community of friars as a diocesan religious community.*

O'Connor. By May of 1999, our numbers were large enough for us to become a diocesan religious institute. The ceremony was held at Saint Patrick's Cathedral with a magnificent and joyous Mass offered by the Cardinal. All the professed friars came before him in the sanctuary, where they made public vows. The Cardinal was in great humor that day and congratulated us warmly. A large number of priests and religious from the archdiocese joined more than a thousand laypeople at what the diocesan newspaper called a most unusual ceremony—the establishment of a religious order at a time when so many communities were in decline.

OUTREACH AND OVERSEAS MISSIONS

Shortly after the formal establishment of the community, a chapter was held in June, at which Father Glenn was elected servant and Father Bob vicar. By that time we were making progress in establishing the community outside the United States.

During the jubilee year of 2000, we opened a mission at Comayagua, Honduras, an ancient, very poor city, which was chosen because of our friendship with the Franciscan Sisters of the Immaculate Conception from Mexico. They have helped us over the years in many essential ways. This community, which was founded in the nineteenth century, has several thousand members, and we were fortunate enough to have the former provincial, Sister Imelda, as the superior of the sisters in New York. They suggested Comayagua, and since our establishment there, our mission has grown and prospered with the encouragement of Bishop Gerald Scarpone, O.F.M.

Because of our connection with Youth 2000, we also had a number of English brothers and felt at that time that we should make an opening in England, where Youth 2000 had begun. In the jubilee year, Bishop Thomas McMahon of Brentwood offered us a small but attractive house with a chapel in a poor section of East London known as Canning Town. The brothers there, led by Brother John Paul Antoine Ouellette, have worked largely with the homeless and have engaged in preaching, especially to the young. England has become very secularized, and during our first weeks the friars were greeted with eggs, rocks, and other insults. However, over time, the brothers have been well received. Outside our neighborhood there is frequent mockery of the religious habit, but Christians at least welcomed us appropriately. The London house is called Saint Fidelis's Friary, and the neighborhood reminds one of those described in the novels of Charles Dickens. The buildings in this neighborhood, however, are only about fifty years old, as the area had been bombed to ashes during the Second World War.

Also in the year 2000, Father Glenn opened the Casa Juan Diego in Yonkers, near two of our friaries. This is a drop-in center originally meant for workers from other countries, especially Mexico. However, poor day laborers, numerous in Yonkers, come there during the day to have a meal, sit and talk, and attend classes to learn how to do various things that are part of American life.

Brothers Leo, Francis, and Martin made their final vows in that year, also; and the community mourned the death of its canonical founder, Cardinal O'Connor.

Cardinal O'Connor had the greatest respect for religious life and had himself gone through the process of beginning the new religious community of the Sisters of Life. Because of our zeal for poverty, the Friars of the Renewal often look a bit disheveled: this is seen as a closer imitation of

MAY 2002: *Ordination at Saint Patrick's Cathedral. On the right are Fathers Thomas and Angelus, kneeling during the ceremony with the other members of the class from Saint Joseph's Seminary, Dunwoodie.*

Saint Francis. Tattered habits with rough hems and a spot here or there characterize the friars' appearance. The Cardinal, once a naval officer, wanted everybody to be dressed with spit and polish, as the saying goes. It is to his great merit that he never corrected us for our homely ways. I don't think he ever entirely understood the particular roughness and simplicity of the friars, but he very much appreciated and defended the sincerity of our religious life.

In May of 2000, Bishop Edward Egan became Archbishop (later Cardinal) of New York. On the day of his installation, Madison Avenue, the street behind the cathedral, was closed to traffic. Hundreds of people gathered there to welcome their new shepherd. As I stood on the steps of the cathedral, I was surprised to see so many Friars and Sisters of the Renewal in gray habits, and the Sisters of Life and the Missionaries of Charity in their white ones. They were all quite noticeable. One of the tabloids even featured a full-page photo of a group of young friars walking through the streets on their way to the cathedral. I could not help think-ing: *A new day is dawning, by the grace of God.*

In 2001, we reached a point of stability. The memory of the friars who had left receded into the distance. Father Fidelis was ordained to the priesthood, and Brothers John Anthony Boughton, Sylvester Mary Mann, John Paul Antoine Ouellette, Anthony Marie Baetzold, Thomas Joseph McGrinder, Luke Mary Fletcher, Crispin Mary Rinaldi, and Juniper Mary Sistare made their final vows. In June a very impressive photograph appeared in *Catholic New York* showing the brothers making their profession. Again it was a newsworthy item.

HERMITAGE AND RETREAT

Over the years, the friars had enjoyed the quiet of the Schenk farm and its rugged simplicity. In October 2001, the new Saint Francis Hermitage officially opened, in Monticello, New York. It was large enough for us to hold our annual community retreat there. The friars will be forever grate-ful to Rita Woodford and Cathy Hickey for making possible our new retreat. Rita gave the sixty acres and houses, which she had always hoped would be a retreat for traditional religious. When she expressed this hope to Father John Lynch, a former member of our community and then assistant in her parish, he introduced her to the Friars of the Renewal. Father John also undertook the rather arduous task of coordinating in our name the construction that was needed to bring this retreat center into being. The work was carried out by a local man, Ray Mickelson, who will always be remembered for his skill and craftsmanship. Cathy Hickey generously provided the funds to purchase the house that is now used by the Sisters of the Renewal.

In 2002, Brothers Angelus and Thomas were ordained priests, and the largest group ever to make final vows were professed on June 9: Brothers Ephrem Ali, Joseph Mary Deane, Juan Diego Sutherland, Peter Marie Westall, Christopher Paul Metzger, Leopold Maria Bokulich, Felix Mary Desilets, and Maximilian Mary Stelmachowski. That same month, Father Glenn was reelected community servant, with Father Richard as the vicar. During this time Father Robert and Brother Michael established a small residence named for Saint Juan Diego in Albuquerque, New Mexico, where they hope eventually to open a friary with an apostolate to the poor.

Our mission in Honduras, now under the leadership of Father Herald and with the assistance of Brothers Felix, Matteo, Damiano Maria Vaissade, and Nathanael Mary Lysinger, continued to make amazing progress. This small group of men was able to establish a center for medical assistance; and a fine group of doctors who belong to Light of the World Charities have been coming to Comayagua to do surgery and other important procedures free of charge. They had not had adequate medical facilities on-site, and the local municipal hospital left much to be desired. The friars therefore opened San Benito Jose Center, with its four operating rooms and sixteen rooms for patients. The day after the medical center was dedicated, hundreds came for free medical assistance. The hospital and the surgeons who go there tend to specialize in general and plastic surgery, urology, gynecology, podiatry, and eye surgery. In Latin America, there is a widespread problem with people with cleft palates and severely misshapen jaw structure. Many children also have clubfeet, which means that they must limp through life if not treated. Friends from around the United States assisted the friars in opening this beautiful center, as well as construction of the Casa Guadalupe, where volunteers will be able to stay at the mission.

Surprisingly, the friars were beginning to become well known in the United States, largely the effect of the Catholic television network EWTN, which regularly featured Father Andrew and me. As a result of our writing and preaching, we both became well known; and because we look so much alike, people often confuse one of us for the other. One friar who has not been confused with anyone else is Father Stan, who is well known through his popular music, which appeals especially to younger Catholics. Father Stan's unique style and personal ability to keep an audience of hundreds of teenagers in rapt attention have made him well known throughout the United States and in other countries.

The preaching apostolate has grown, and a mission team has been established under the direction of Father Mariusz Koch. The friars conduct parish missions and do many kinds of preaching and evangelization throughout the United States and abroad.

Perhaps surprisingly, one of the places where the friars have taken on preaching engagements is Ireland, although we do not have a house there. Through the influence of Brother Columba Maria Jordan, the first

At the Metropolitan Museum of Art, New York, to view an exhibit of Franciscan art, with Archduke Geza von Habsburg, our volunteer guide

Irish member of our community, we were able to get a number of preaching assignments in the Irish Republic and in Northern Ireland. They met with completely unexpected enthusiasm. Priests had warned us that because of the religious crisis in Ireland, we would preach to empty churches. Nothing could have been further from the truth. Apart from an occasional nasty remark in the street because we wear our habits in public, the Irish people have welcomed the friars warmly.

The young friars recently began an apostolate called the Catholic Underground, which meets monthly at Saint John Baptist Church in Yonkers. The evening begins with a Eucharistic holy hour, followed by music, featuring a Catholic musician, or another form of Catholic culture. Meanwhile there is an opportunity for confession and friendly interchange. The program is a response to Pope John Paul II's request that we Catholics engage and Christianize the culture we live in. It is a popular program, and each month the hall is packed to the doors.

In May 2003, the friars had their largest ordination class: Fathers Sylvester, Joseph, Luke, and Juniper. Seven brothers also made final vows that year: Father Mariusz Koch, and Brothers Sharbel Miriam Alkhass, Lawrence Joseph Schroedel, Matteo Marie Dengler, Jacob Marie Hausman, Emmanuel Mary Mansford, and Gabriel Mary Bakkar.[12] The sisters also opened their second house at the convent of Saint Francis Xavier parish in the Bronx and reestablished their convent of Our Lady of Guadalupe. Happily, the sisters now have three members finally professed: Sisters Lucille, Regina Economopoulos, and Clare Matthiass. There are also five temporarily professed members: Sisters Francis Teresa O'Donnell, Agnes Mary Holtz, Cecilia Francis Jesse, Jacinta Maria Pollard, and Miriam Thérèse Johnson.[13]

Again we experienced the problem of not being able to fit everybody in. While we were trying to decide where we should go next, a beautiful old convent that had belonged to cloistered Dominican nuns became available in Newark, New Jersey. The 125-year-old monastery was the oldest house of contemplative Dominicans nuns in the United States. It

---

[12] One of the good difficulties of writing the history of our new community is that it quickly becomes outdated, with a number of friars entering each year who will play a significant role in opening new friaries and establishing new apostolates. Among the newer friars it is interesting to note how many came from other countries. Besides those already mentioned, as of August 2005, finally professed friars include: Brothers Gerard Matthias Kanapesz, Paulus Maria Tautz (Germany), Benedict Joseph Maria Delarmi (England), Dominic Miriam Bormans (New Zealand), Francis Mary Roaldi, Solanus Maria Benfatti, Pio Maria Hoffman, Agostino Miguel Torres, Augustine Mary Conner (England), Damiano Maria Vaissade, Isaac Mary Spinharney, Simon Marie Dankoski, and Albert Maria Osewski (Poland).

Temporary professed brothers include: Father Raphael Jacques Chilou (France); and Brothers Samuel Nix, Louis Marie Leonelli, Daniel Marie Williamson, Philip Maria Allen, Nathaniel Mary Lysinger, Columba Maria Jordan (Ireland), Thomas More Noble, John Bosco Mills (England), Youssef Mariam Hanna (Lebanon), Giuseppe Maria Siniscalchi, Charles Benoît Rèche (France), Bonaventure Mary Rummell (Germany), Séraphim Marie Roycourt (France), Jeremiah Myriam Shryock, Christian Marie Oppe, Honorat Maria Grifka, David Mary Valenzuela, Joachim Joseph Bellavance, Sebastian Maria Kajko (Poland), Tobias Joseph Holtz, Paschal Maria Colby, Antonio Maria Diez de Medina, and Paul Raniero Donnelly.

Our novices are: Father Paul DaDamio, Brothers Christopher Joseph McBride (England), Patrick Crowley (Ireland), Andrew Maria Corsini, Ignatius Joseph DiGirolamo, Dismas Marie Kline, Mariano Joseph Demma, Gregory Bottaro, and Luke Joseph Leighton. Transfer religious and candidates for postulancy include: Father Grzegorz Wierzba, O.F.M., Brother John Brice, O.F.M., Patrick Long, Jose Arroyo, Jason White, Paul Thomas, Chris Leonard, Tony Alarcon, Julio de Jesus, Augustine Shim, Chris Johannssen, Paul Kim, and Christopher Kyte.

Another change from our general chapter in June 2005 is that Father Bernard Murphy is now our Community Servant, the first nonfounder to be elected to that position. Father Glenn, who wrote the Preface to this book, completed his second three-year term in that office.

[13] The Sisters of the Renewal currently have five novices: Sisters Margaret Mary Hegarty, Veronica Marie Vandenbunder, Elizabeth Marie Hogan, Catherine Mary Holum, and Francesca Maria Sabo.

was attractive to us because it was located in one of the poorer sections of Newark, a city that has seen a great deal of violence and difficulty over the years. We were very grateful to Archbishop John Myers of Newark for directly assisting us in obtaining this convent, as well as to a group of generous friends who serve as the board of directors and own the building. Because the sisters who had lived at the monastery and for generations had spent their lives in perpetual adoration, we decided to call the house Most Blessed Sacrament Friary. Father Bernard, the novice master, and our novices moved into the friary in March 2004.

A SERIOUS ACCIDENT

In January 2004, in Orlando, Florida, I was struck as a pedestrian by a car and came very close to death on three occasions. I had traveled to Florida, accompanied by Father John Lynch and David Burns, to teach at a renewal program for priests. Father Lynch and David prayed at my side for the first few days until a number of friars, led by Father Glenn, were able to get to the hospital. They stayed on for weeks. A surprising response came from people throughout the United States and other countries in the form of fifty thousand e-mails and thousands of get-well cards. As I continue to recover, the friars recognize that the Lord has used this event in order to make our renewal better known.

A NEW POPE

In April 2005, a great sorrow came to the Catholic Church and to the Friars and Sisters of the Renewal. Almost all of the friars had lived their teenage and adult lives in the pontificate of John Paul II. After a long period of illness, during which he bravely struggled, the great Pope went to his eternal reward. During his last illness the community began a vigil of prayer, with the friars and sisters keeping watch in prayer during the night and day. In that way our community accompanied our dear Holy Father on his journey. There is no doubt that as the Friars and Sisters of the Renewal grow, the impact of the pontificate of this great man will continue. He inspired and guided us in innumerable ways, and we were filled with joy at various times to have met him.

After the death of the Pope we continued our vigils and hours of adoration, praying for the conclave of cardinals that would elect his successor. It was with great joy and satisfaction that we heard of Cardinal Joseph Ratzinger's election as Pope Benedict XVI. Some of us had met the cardinal during his years in the Curia. During that period I had the opportunity of informing him of the progress of our community, writing to him for that purpose just two months before his election. He was very familiar with the Bavarian Capuchins, so he was fascinated to learn of what we were trying to do and our intention of preserving the Capuchin ideal and identity.

FORMING COMMUNITY TRADITIONS

We have spoken about the general trends in our young community—the need for quiet and for contemplative prayer, the pro-life work, and the work with youths, especially in the Youth 2000 movement. There are a few other things that must be spoken of here.

In the chapels of our friaries, we insist on austerity and a minimum of decoration. The only artistic representations permitted are the San Damiano crucifix above the altar and a picture of Our Lady of Guadalupe. This austerity of imagery is intended to direct our attention, and our devotion, to Christ, especially in the mystery of His Sacred Heart and the Divine Mercy. There has always been an explicit and warm devotion to the Mother of Jesus Christ, the Blessed Virgin Mary. Many of the friars have followed the European custom of including the name of Mary in one form or another in their own religious name. Also, the Rosary is one of our important daily devotions, and there is great love for and familiarity with the Blessed Mother in our community. There is a sense of the vital presence of the Mother of God, as well as of Saint Joseph, Saint Francis, and Saint Clare.

In the midst of community life—whether on an apostolic day, when an endless number of people come and there is a swirl of activity around the friary door, or on a Friday, when we try to maintain a time of quiet recollection—there is one element that can be perceived only through quiet waiting and watching. This is the presence of Our Lord Jesus Christ. Everyone in the two communities is seeking not only to imitate Christ and follow His Gospel teachings but also to know and love Him. Like all Christians, we are vitally aware that He is the vine and we are the branches. The friars, sisters, and their associates seek to have in them that mind which was in Christ Jesus (see Philippians 2:5). As you review this book with its striking pictures, please pray for us and for the whole Church that Christ may come and live within us all.

Devotion to our blessed Savior, especially in the Eucharistic presence, is the most obvious element binding the community together. In times of confusion and collapse, it is important to keep in mind that this thriving community is centered entirely on Jesus Christ, in daily union with His Sacrifice, in devout Communion with Him, and in adoration of His sacramental presence.

The Franciscan Friars and Sisters of the Renewal—
following the General Chapter in June 2005.

FRANCISCAN LIFE AND APOSTOLATES

by

THE FRIARS AND SISTERS OF THE RENEWAL

I

THE JOYFUL MYSTERIES

Each vocation story is a unique glimpse of a joyful mystery: that God calls us to join in His work. Each one requires that "Fiat" or "Amen" to His call. Brother Youssef Mariam (pictured here) explains how our Lady helped him to say yes.

1. *The Annunciation*

"Mary said, '. . . let it be to me according to your word.' "

LUKE 1:38

VOCATION—MARY

Having been born in Lebanon, a country full of fear and war and power outages, I took hope from candles—a worldly, temporary hope—in my attempt to escape the darkness. After I moved to Canada, the light of candles, even those used on dinner tables, became a sad reminder of destruction, fear, and death. When I saw the sky filled with light from fireworks, the accompanying loud noise made me think of the explosion of bombs.

For thirty-five years I had been looking for the temporary, worldly light that does not last. The light of this world can be decorative without meaning and can give little joy, happiness, or peace. It is like a beautiful rose without fragrance or a decorated candle without light.

Before falling in love with God, I was like someone carrying an unlighted candle in the dark places of the world; it could do no good for me or for others. During my darkest night I met a beautiful woman, who was tender, loving, sweet, and compassionate. She stopped me and asked if I would light my candle in order to see the way to God and to be a light to God for others. The loving, tender woman was Mary, the virgin Mother of God. My yes to her question gave me lasting hope, peace, and love of God and His creatures.

After more than a year of saying yes to God, the Holy Spirit spoke to me one day at work, clearly telling me to leave my work and serve only the Lord. With tears I said yes again, not knowing where my assent would lead me. After discussing my vocation, I found peace with the Franciscan Friars of the Renewal. When I was asked to choose a religious name, I decided to add Mariam (Mary in Arabic) to my name in order to honor Our Lady, my Mother and the Mother of Jesus, and remind me always of her love, compassion, and prayers.

— BR. YOUSSEF MARIAM HANNA

Franciscan Sisters also are not born as sisters except in the eyes of the Lord, who reveals His call when He wills. Sister Regina Marie is seen here at her first profession of vows.

VOCATION

I never would have thought that living a simple life, having nothing of my own, being totally God's and giving up my own self-will with the Franciscan Sisters of the Renewal would bring such joy. Thirteen years ago I was a bartender and a pool shark. I thought I had it all, but there was an emptiness in my heart. I was trying to fill it with the things of the world, not of God. I was twenty-four years old when I came to know Jesus through the suffering and death of my mother. I was lost when she died. Through prayer and suffering I found life in Christ.

In August 1993, I first met the Sisters and Friars of the Renewal. I saw young women and men giving their lives to God, having nothing and being so joyful. Their joy was real, and that is what I was searching for. With God's grace I entered the order in January 1997. Since then I have experienced the Franciscan joy that comes from embracing all, having nothing, and being willing to suffer for the love of Christ.

On August 2, 2003, I professed my final vows. My joy was great as I became the spouse of Christ forever and gave my life to Him and for His people. I thank God for my holy Franciscan calling, for the grace and joy He gives me to live this life. I ask for your prayers and God's grace to be faithful, steadfast in His love, and to embrace all with joy and generosity.

— SR. REGINA MARIE ECONOMOPOULOS

The call of Abraham took him far from his native land.
Many of our friars and sisters have made similar journeys in their vocations,
following the Lord with headlights but without a road map. Brother Dominic,
photographed here with national pride at the World Youth Day in Toronto,
brings some "thunder from down under" to the Bronx.

VOCATION

The flag you see is the pride of the Commonwealth. The four stars represent the Southern Cross, the constellation that guided my forefathers to the shores of the Great White Cloud, as New Zealand is affectionately called by the natives. The Union Jack in the upper-right corner reminds me of my country's allegiance to Her Majesty the Queen of England. "Oh, close to my soul are the stars of my homeland, New Zealand."

As evident in the cultural diversity of our community, we friars hail from many parts of the world. The various nationalities represented in our community are manifested in the mix of personalities. The call to religious life, God's inner call, was subtle for me. It came through a low-key, yet intense conversion while serving in the New Zealand Army. From that experience God led me across the Pacific to this land.

When Jesus invited me to follow Him in a more absolute manner, He led me to the stigmatized arms of Saint Francis, who is so well emulated in this community. I recently made my final vows. Praised be Jesus Christ!

— Br. Dominic Miriam Bormans

2. *The Visitation*

"In those days Mary arose and went with haste into the hill country,
to a city of Judah, and she entered the house of Zechariah and
greeted Elizabeth."

LUKE 1:39

PRO-LIFE

In the face of every child we must see the face of Christ Jesus our Lord. Life and death hang in the balance on the streets of Manhattan. We see the face of fear and despair in each mother and father who approach the abortion clinic. Our hope is that the face of life will bring trust to those who are constantly facing fear and despair. We bring a presence of prayer, peaceful conversation, and display of holy images to help the people on the street awaken from the slumber of self-interest.

When we become conscious of the face of Christ, we find our whole existence in His life and the life of all humanity. This compels us to make a choice: Will we turn to His merciful Face or turn away in denial of His suffering Body?

— BR. MARTIN DE PORRES ERVIN

Brother Martin de Porres (top), shown with an unmistakable message, and the other friars know that their work concerns the spiritual life of the parents as well as the physical life of their children. Praying and counseling on the front lines at abortion sites is part of our hands-on work with the poor. Here Brother Leo joins a group praying near an abortuary on Park Avenue in Manhattan.

Father Richard (top), at a Lenten meal with the postulants, explains the first stage of formation in our community, which lasts for approximately six months. At the end of this time, if there is a mutual agreement that the Lord is calling the candidate to our life, he or she is invested with the habit as a novice.
Brother Matteo is shown receiving the habit (bottom).

3. *The Nativity*

"I was nursed with care in swaddling cloths."

WISDOM 7:4

POSTULANCY

What is a postulant? A postulant is a creature who asks a lot of questions. The Latin word *postulare* means "to question." Since this is the first stage of life in our religious community, a postulant has many little questions, such as "What page does Morning Prayer begin on?" or "How do I get that spaghetti stain off my white shirt?" More important questions are on his mind as well, sometimes asking the Lord, "Please teach me to pray", or the simple rhetorical prayer of Saint Francis, "O Lord, who art Thou and what am I?"

Of course, the main question of postulancy is, "Is the Lord really calling me here?" It is usually followed by "Can I really do this?" A postulant director, therefore, is a creature who prays for a lot of patience!

One of the benefits of being the postulant director is that postulants often enter with a holy zeal and generous enthusiasm that is contagious. They remind me of the flame that I felt in my heart during my time of discernment whenever I heard the words of Jesus, "If any man would come after me, let him deny himself and take up his cross daily and follow me" (Luke 9:23).

As the early Capuchin Franciscans wrote about "eating the sins of the people" by uniting themselves with the Lord in a life of penance, so the postulants have many opportunities to test their generosity and increase their gift of themselves to the Lord. For example, when I gave them a number of possibilities of what we might be able to do together during Lent and asked which ones they thought would be helpful, their response was more or less a desire to do them all!

Ancient philosophers taught that the unquestioned life is not worth living. All of us are to be postulants in some way. No matter what our vocation, we can gratefully ask the Lord, "How can I serve You more generously?" Our heavenly Director delights in hearing that question!

—Fr. Richard Roemer

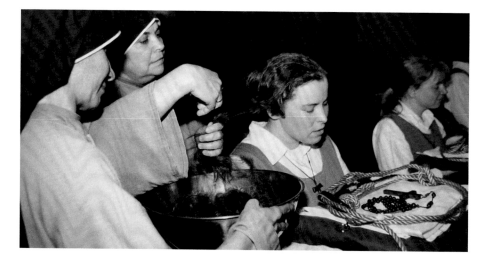

Some moments of the Drama of Reform are particularly dramatic, such as the change of appearance at investiture. Here, Sister Jacinta, with Sister Miriam in the background, allows her hair to be cut by Sister Lucille prior to being invested with the habit and veil.

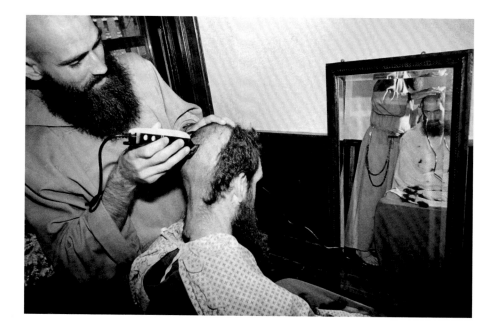

The first question (spoken or not) most people have when they see the friars has something to do with our beards. The Constitutions of the early Capuchin Franciscans, from whom we take our rugged appearance, describe the beard as something "severe, austere, manly, natural, and despised". It can be related to the vow of poverty in its natural simplicity, to obedience in our sharing a corporate identity, and to chastity as a permanent sign that we are "not available". Brother Columba Maria, getting his hair cut by Brother Pio, gives us an account of a similar sign of taking on a new identity.

NEW IDENTITY

One day, when I was eighteen, I was at Mass in my parish and heard a reading taken from the Acts of the Apostles. It ended with the sentence: "At Cenchreae [Paul] cut his hair, for he had made a vow" (Acts 18:18).

I was not at all pleased to hear this particular reading. At the time, I had shoulder-length curly hair, to which I was very attached. Too attached. As I left the church that morning, I knew that God wanted me to do something drastic about it. After a few pained days attempting to haggle with the Lord for a lower price, I finally gave in and decided to shave all my locks. I was very surprised to feel a great sense of peace and freedom after I had made this choice.

As a friar, I am not required to shave my head. In fact, our Constitutions state only that "the friars are encouraged to have a plain beard". There could be a temptation to shave it off just because most of the other brothers do, but I try to connect it with my experience as a vain eighteen-year-old. Shaving my head is a small but powerful way of denying myself, taking up my cross, and following Jesus Christ as Saint Francis did. Perhaps in that first call to shave my head and leave behind something the world holds dear, God was preparing me for the utter renunciation of my own will that this Franciscan life requires.

More than ever, I now feel the peace and freedom that only Jesus can give.

— Br. Columba Maria Jordan

Father Bernard, the novice director, sends the novices out with his blessing (above), and directs them in their studies (below). Brother Thomas More (seated at the far right, below), a widower and an experienced lawyer, found the novitiate studies much less intense than his law school courses.

NOVITIATE STUDIES

In their studies before making temporary vows, novices examine the nature of vows under canon law, Church teachings about the essentials of religious life, the psychology of spiritual development, Franciscan history and writings, and the community's constitutions and norms. As in their previous studies as postulants, their efforts receive support from the community's strong prayer life and its faithfulness to Church teachings. Some will later pursue seminary studies leading to ordination to the priesthood, while others may take classes as lay brothers. The community encourages studies based on its needs and a particular friar's interests and talents.

Such learning has been a blessing to the community. Some people, accustomed to society's secular thinking, consider any academic program that is so rooted in prayer to be quaint and even intellectually suspect. Such a view was expressed to one of our friars in an e-mail message from a friend before he came to the community. Noting the past academic honors and career accomplishments of the future friar, the author of the e-mail predicted that the community could not satisfy such love of learning. The writer conceded that the community seemed prayerful enough, and ended with the blunt question: "What do you have in common with Padre Pio?"

Years earlier this future friar had pursued theological studies, which were tainted by false teaching. Being without much spiritual support, he began to question numerous Church doctrines and event to doubt God's existence. Fortunately, he later developed a strong love for the Church and a deep desire to help himself and others to draw closer to God. His reply to the e-mail stated: "I'm sure that you're right. I still don't have enough in common with Padre Pio. To make up for that failing, I'm going to accept God's invitation to join this community."

— Br. Thomas More Noble

Brother Giuseppe Maria writes about other varied experiences of the novitiate year.
Since the time of his writing, our novitiate has moved to Most Blessed Sacrament Friary in Newark, New Jersey.
Saint Joseph's Friary is now home to our postulants. Here Brother Giuseppe Maria takes a break
from his cooking responsibilities to feed and pray with one of our neighbors.

NOVITIATE—FOOD MINISTRY

Flowers, steel security grates, prayers, and peanut butter and jelly sandwiches comprise the life of a novice in Harlem. Through the doors of Saint Joseph's Friary pass the lives of the friars in training. Amid the darkness of poverty, violence, drugs, and despair, the novitiate stands as an oasis of hope, light, safety, and love. The prayerful presence of our novices deep in the inner city brings a soothing balm to a world that is often threatening and uncertain. Following the example of Saint Francis, the novices strive to live a genuine love for all God's creation, especially the poor.

The brother novices rush out these doors to attend class with Father Benedict, Father Andrew, and others. They also leave this sanctuary of prayer to bring Christ's love to the darkness of an abortion mill in Manhattan, to disadvantaged and troubled boys at Children's Village, and to the streets of Harlem. Through the same doors flow a constant stream of visitors and the generosity of the countless benefactors who make our life possible.

The generosity of our benefactors allows us to feed the hungry in our neighborhood. We offer peanut butter and jelly sandwiches (usually two) to those who come in search of food. Along with the sandwiches we offer a hot drink, plus a prayer and a kind word or two. Frequently the prayer and encouragement offer more comfort and satisfaction than the sandwiches.

Those who come to our door are hungry for more than bodily food; like everyone everywhere, they hunger for the love of God.

— Br. Giuseppe Maria Siniscalchi

Saint Francis taught us that everything we do must be subservient to the spirit of prayer and devotion.
The time of novitiate is meant to instill in us a lifelong habit of prayer in imitation of Our Lady.
Sister Agnes Mary is shown in a quiet moment with the Lord.

NOVITIATE—PRAYER

HAIL, MARY, FULL OF GRACE . . . Mary, you are all holy and most beautiful among women. You radiate Christ in your very being. The angel Gabriel came to you and announced that you would give birth to Jesus, conceiving Him by the power of the Holy Spirit. Your response was, "Behold, I am the handmaid of the Lord; let it be to me according to your word." May every moment of each day be an imitation of your *fiat*. Please take my imperfect prayer and present it to your Son, because I know He cannot refuse His Mother.

As one of the novices in the Franciscan Sisters of the Renewal, I am growing in a more intimate relationship with Christ, preparing to become His spouse. We do this by living the life, through study and prayer, which includes daily Mass, an hour of silent meditation, the liturgy of the hours, Eucharistic adoration, and a great love for and devotion to our Lady. It is through continuous dialogue with Jesus that this love grows, and it is the spouse of the Holy Spirit who teaches us to ponder Him in our hearts day and night.

— SR. AGNES MARY HOLTZ

4. *The Presentation*

"[T]hey brought him up to Jerusalem to present him to the Lord . . . and to offer a sacrifice."

LUKE 2:22, 24

PROFESSION

On August 31, 2003, I took my final vows, committing myself to Christ and His Church and promising to be poor, chaste, and obedient for the rest of my life. I became a Franciscan Friar of the Renewal forever!

Through my promise of poverty, I will never be paid for what I do; our retirement plan is eternal life! Our Lord told the rich young man in the Gospel (Matthew 19:21): "If you would be perfect, go, sell what you possess and give to the poor, and you will have treasure in heaven; and come, follow me." As for the reward for those who follow Him, Jesus says: "And every one who has left houses or brothers or sisters or father or mother or children or lands, for my name's sake, will receive a hundredfold, and inherit eternal life" (Matthew 19:29–30).

During my time in temporary vows, I prayed and discerned whether I should dedicate my life to God through a vow of perpetual chastity. I had thought about settling down, getting married, raising a family . . . However, I didn't feel called to marriage. Having recognized that I had been given a special gift from God to live my vocation within the Franciscan Order, I just knew that I was supposed to be a Franciscan Friar of the Renewal. Our Lord tells us in the same chapter of Saint Matthew's Gospel: "He who is able to receive this, let him receive it" (19:12)

Through my vow of obedience, I regard my local servant (superior) as my "boss". It is he who manifests God's will in my life through his running the day-to-day operations of the friary. Jesus told us of the importance and closeness to Him of all who do His heavenly Father's will (see Matthew 12:50).

In taking final vows, I believe I fulfilled God's eternal will for me. I prayed for those who made profession with me that we would all receive the grace necessary to live the life to which God had called us. It seemed that my whole life, my whole existence, was coming to an end—and was beginning at the same time. The period of discernment was past; my life as a professed member of the community was beginning.

The moment I made my profession, I felt great peace and couldn't stop smiling from ear to ear. I had received abundant grace through our Lady's intercession and the power of the Holy Spirit. I thank God for the gift of my vocation and for guiding me through the five years of testing and discernment.

— Br. Jacob Marie Hausman

Pope John Paul II once said that the liturgical feast of the Presentation especially reminds us of those who make an offering of themselves to the Lord through the consecrated life. Brother Jacob is shown making his vows to Father Glenn, as Father Benedict witnesses and Brother Leo assists.

PROFESSION

Profession of final vows is an extraordinary event in the life of a religious. After the brother has publicly made his vows during the Mass of profession and signed the necessary documentation, the Community Servant offers a closing prayer of consecration.

Many people contribute to making a Mass of final profession such a beautiful event. One of these is the master of ceremonies, whose job it is to coordinate the entire liturgy. Everyone knows he is there doing his job, but his presence should fade into the background.

In these pictures of profession liturgies, the master of ceremonies is not the focal point, nor should he be. A master of ceremonies is hardly to be noticed; he coordinates but never dominates. All those present are drawn into the beauty of the profession Mass as they witness a life being given to God in love.

— Br. Leo Joseph Fisher

We all received the call to holiness at our Baptism. We were each cleansed from sin and set apart for God as His adopted children. Religious profession, through the evangelical counsels of poverty, chastity, and obedience, is a deepening of this baptismal consecration, although it is also a new and special consecration itself. Through vows, we religious profess to live out our baptismal call in an intense and radical way, not only by following Christ but also by living the same lifestyle He lived on earth. Through our consecration we proclaim publicly the primacy and absoluteness of God: He is first and He is all.

Through poverty we let go of all that disappoints and decays, forsaking worldly wealth for the real riches found only in Christ. Through chastity we forgo the love of one imperfect man for the love of the one Perfect Man. And by loving Jesus with an undivided heart we receive the grace to love others more, not less. When we profess obedience, we give God the only thing that is truly ours to give; we freely offer Him our will. Each vow is motivated by love for Him who loved us first.

The rite of religious profession within Mass is a serious and solemn moment as the young religious kneels, placing her hands in those of her superior, and solemnly making her vows before God and His Church. Her head is then veiled in black and crowned with white flowers. She turns to face the congregation, and the solemnity is broken with the joyful applause of those present in gratitude for another soul given completely to God. As the celebration continues, the newly professed receives the *embratio*, or fraternal embrace, of every Franciscan present. "Welcome, spouse of Christ," the profession liturgy seems to say, "to the royal road of following the poor Christ in the footsteps of the Poverello!"

— SR. FRANCIS TERESA

Another powerful moment at final profession is the praying of the litany of the saints, during which the friars being professed lie prostrate on the floor, and we call on our "friends in high places" for their support. Brother Leo, who has often served as the liturgical master of ceremonies, reminds us of the fraternal support that is experienced in many ways at the Mass of profession.

Sister Francis Teresa is shown exchanging the white veil of a novice for the black veil of a professed sister. She gives us her reflections on what these vows mean for her as a Sister of the Renewal.

5. *The Finding in the Temple*

"And Jesus increased in wisdom and in stature, and in favor with
God and man."

LUKE 2:52

APOSTOLATE TO YOUTH

Jesus, the divine Son of God, had no confusion about who He was. His
priority of being found "in my Father's house" (Luke 2:49) was merely
highlighted by the fact that He had the two greatest parents ever. And let
us not forget that Jesus caused them "great anxiety". Nonetheless, the
divine mission, which climaxed with His passion, death, and Resurrection, had its humble beginnings in Nazareth, where "He was obedient to
them". There was no confusion about His identity or His mission.

The children of the South Bronx, unfortunately, often do not have
that certainty of their identity and mission. Family breakdown, aided by a
culture of death, has wreaked havoc on our younger brothers and sisters,
leaving them utterly confused and disillusioned in their priorities. Drug
abuse, gang violence, sexual promiscuity, and absent parents have all
caused the young to lose their way to their "Father's house".

Saint Francis Youth Center is a gift from the heart of the Child Jesus.
Begun in 1993, the Center has become a refuge, a house where God is the
Father of the poor. The Youth Center sponsors summer camps, after-
school programs, retreats, Eucharistic adoration, cultural enrichment programs, and athletic programs. There the brokenness is healed, sins are
forgiven, the joy of being young is restored, and the lost are found in their
"Father's house".

— BR. THOMAS JOSEPH MCGRINDER

*Brother Thomas Joseph (top) is with a happy young man at our summer
program in the Bronx, while Brother Shawn Conrad and Brother John
Paul help with batting practice (bottom). A gymnasium may not look like
the Temple of Jerusalem, but the young people in the South Bronx call it
"the Church". Brother Thomas, who coordinates our Youth for Christ
program, tells us more.*

As we move from Jesus' childhood to His public ministry, we cannot forget that our Lord most likely spent most of His adult life working in a humble, hidden manner with His parents at Nazareth. Brother Honorat Maria, shown here, another carpenter's son, writes about this essential part of our lives.

"Is not this the carpenter, the son of Mary and brother of James . . . ?"

MARK 6:3

MANUAL LABOR

After Saint Francis's conversion, Jesus told him, "Rebuild my Church, which as you can see is falling into ruin." Singing hymns and prayers, Francis begged for stones and mortar and repaired three churches. Then Christ asked him to do more—to rebuild not only buildings but the faith of God's people, the Church.

Manual labor remains an important part of our lives today. Saint Francis asked the brothers to use their talents and trades to serve Christ. From a young age I started learning from my father, who is a carpenter. Every summer I worked with him and also earned a college degree in civil engineering. Now part of my service to the Lord is to use the construction experience that I learned through the love and patience of my father.

Our focus on manual labor fulfills Jesus' great commandment: to love God and our neighbor. We maintain the buildings and other material gifts God has provided for our use and entrusted to our care. It is a great joy to provide safe, prayerful buildings for our brothers and those we serve.

Even when Saint Francis came upon a poorly cared-for church in his later years, he picked up a broom—and taught his followers to do the same. We strive to follow the example of Saint Francis, the rebuilder of holy Mother Church, who never extinguished a spirit of prayer and devotion.

— Br. Honorat Maria Grifka

Brother Charles Benoît, shown rebuilding a friary wall, is from northern France and adds his sense of the beauté *of manual work.*

MANUAL LABOR

The friars do as much of the maintenance work in our houses as possible, for practical and economic reasons, as well as for spiritual ones. In our work we imitate Jesus and His foster father, Saint Joseph, who worked with their hands. It is also a way to be close to the poor, who do manual work primarily.

The most important point is that manual labor involves the body, so it is a beautiful way to worship God with our whole being. As Saint Francis taught us, we can participate in the beauty of creation by our work, provided that we do our best, making everything as beautiful as possible.

— BR. CHARLES BENOÎT RÈCHE

II

THE LUMINOUS MYSTERIES

Sometimes we have the joy of seeing the fruit of our labors with the young people.
Father Thomas gives us the background of this picture.

1. *The Baptism of the Lord*

"Go therefore and make disciples of all nations, baptizing them in
the name of the Father and of the Son and of the Holy Spirit."

MATTHEW 28:19

SACRAMENTS

Receiving the sacraments of Baptism, First Holy Communion, and Confirmation is a common occurrence in any parish church. Why was this celebration special?

Doneil Anthony Alexander had been a regular at our Saint Francis Center since it opened in 1990; the Center offers various programs for youths throughout the week. Doneil (a.k.a. "Sweets") was born and raised in Brooklyn, and when he was ten years old he moved with his family to the Bronx. As a child, he attended a Protestant church, but through the temptations of the street he took some wrong turns in life. As he continued to come to Saint Francis Center, he began to understand that he needed God as a priority in his life.

When the Center began a program for the reception of the sacraments in 2002, Doneil, then 23, was the first to sign up. He had learned that it was only through the life of grace that he could become a mature man of God.

His many years of learning about the Catholic faith, in addition to the seven months of intensive sacramental preparation, reached their fulfillment at Easter 2003, when he took the plunge into the life-giving waters of Baptism. He was also confirmed and received his First Holy Communion at the same time, thus being changed forever.

— FR. THOMAS FRANCIS CACCIOLA

2. The Wedding Feast at Cana

"[T]he mother of Jesus said to him, 'They have no wine.' . . . This, the first of his signs, Jesus did at Cana in Galilee, and manifested his glory; and his disciples believed in him."

JOHN 2:3, 11

PROVIDENCE

With a long list of characters and controversies, Franciscan history reads almost like a comic book. There has been no bigger controversy in the history of the Franciscan Order than the issue of poverty. This vow, which every Catholic religious professes, has been for me an ongoing challenge and a great doorway into gratitude. This gratitude grows in the light of God's Providence. God provides.

The second luminous mystery of the Rosary has helped me understand Saint Francis's love for holy Lady Poverty. I love the mystery of the miracle at the wedding feast of Cana. Jesus is present and concerned about us, even in the smallest things! The miracle at Cana manifests the reality of Divine Providence. "They have no wine. . . . Do whatever he tells you" (John 2:3, 5). God provides.

The vow of poverty has taught me that the ordinary moments of daily life become meaningful. I cannot count the number of times we have experienced this in our Franciscan life. One day, one of our friars was concerned that we had not eaten any fruit or vegetables in a while. One of the brothers jokingly commented that we should ask Saint Thérèse (whom her mother in a letter once called "the little monkey") to send us "bananas from heaven". The next day a vocation candidate showed up unexpectedly at our door with a box of bananas. His opening words were an embarrassed apology: his sister would not let him leave home without the bananas! On another occasion, we were at a remote retreat house. Someone came to the door with an armful of bananas just a minute after we had asked Saint Thérèse to help! God provides, often with a sense of humor.

Choosing to have the minimum rather than the maximum goes against the grain of our American sensibilities. Why would the poor Christ invite us to follow Him in this way? Saint Clare wrote that Jesus calls us to be detached from the things of time in order to be attached to the things of eternity. Holy poverty reminds us of the fact that we are pilgrims on earth. Heaven is our only true home. It also allows Him an opportunity to express His love for us. As we strive to live for God alone, God provides.

The practical day-to-day living of this vow has been a transforming experience. We are in this world, but not of it. To want, to be in need, to be a beggar before God, leads to a deeper awareness of how things really are, of the truth that every good thing is a gift from our heavenly Father. I walk on God's earth, eat God's food, breathe God's air, exist because of God's power. Our very life is grounded in this all-pervasive mystery. God provides.

— Fr. Luke Mary Fletcher

Two novice sisters, Sister Jacinta (above) and Sister Miriam are shown preparing food provided through the generosity of benefactors and volunteers of all ages. Father Luke shares his experience of the Lord's provision.

The Lord's Providence extends far beyond the provision of material goods,
to the provision of people to help us and to be helped.
Sometimes we are like the servants at Cana who filled the jugs with mere water.
We get to see the Lord transform those basic provisions into supernatural goods
that cheer the hearts of His children. Brother Maximilian Mary, shown here helping
a friend from the neighborhood, writes.

PROVISION FOR THE POOR

The poor are not problems to be solved but people to be loved and served. Every week, the friars distribute food to the needy who come to the door of Saint Crispin's Friary. I have been privileged to serve many who might be thought of as "characters", and have built relationships with them of trust, prayer, and friendship.

"If a brother or sister is ill-clad and in lack of daily food, and one of you says to them, 'Go in peace, be warmed and filled,' without giving them the things needed for the body, what does it profit? So faith by itself, if it has no works, is dead" (James 2:15–17).

Bread and vegetables, rice and beans, preaching and prayer, are all given as an expression of our Father's provident love, working through the body of Christ. In exchange for this food, I get a bear hug and laughter from old Pablo, grandmotherly kisses from Olga, volunteer help from Florence and Anna, and so many smiles and thank-yous. There is always work, and it is sometimes heavy and messy, but many hands make light work. Love is given and received, with our eyes on Jesus, in the church and in our needy neighbors, all amid the hustle and bustle of the South Bronx.

— Br. Maximilian Mary Stelmachowski

Our Lady's solidarity with the couple who ran out of wine prompted her to intercede for our Lord's first miracle. Brother Gerard Matthias, pictured here, also experiences the Lord's generosity when serving the poor.

SOLIDARITY WITH THE POOR

This frozen moment of joy, in greeting one of our faithful volunteers and friends, Louis Carillo, prompted me to recall the many blessings of working with and for the poor at La Casa de San Juan Diego, as well as in the streets and byways of southwest Yonkers. I truly need to give thanks to our merciful Savior more often and in better ways.

Our work is not merely social work. To keep our focus, we need to imitate the disciple Mary at the feet of Jesus (see Luke 10:39) so that we can begin to understand the Holy Spirit's prompting and "be filled with the knowledge of his will in all spiritual wisdom and understanding" (Colossians 1:9).

We are all truly called to grow in trust in the beautiful promises of prodigal love the Lord has for each of us so that we can believe, and see, and echo Our Lord's words: "the measure you give will be the measure you get, and still more will be given you" (Mark 4:24).

— Br. Gerard Matthias Kanapesz

3. *The Proclamation of the Kingdom*

"And he called to him the twelve, and began to send them out two by two, and gave them authority..."

MARK 6:7

EVANGELIZATION

For Saint Francis, Jesus was all. The Lord was constantly on his mind, on his lips, and in his heart. It is said that when Saint Francis heard the name of Jesus, he would lick his lips to savor the sweetness of the holy name. He made the Gospel the marrow of his own life and of that of his friars. He firmly believed that Jesus was the Messiah, the Son of the living God, the Savior of the world, the great pearl for which one should sell everything he has in order to obtain it. His love for Christ filled him with zeal to share this Good News with everyone he met, so that they too might come to know the goodness, beauty, and splendor of the Lord. Accordingly, he sent his friars out into the world to proclaim the Gospel with their humble lives and simple words.

God chooses the weak to shame the proud, and He pours forth the richness of His grace into the hearts of those who are poor in spirit. Saint Francis was only one man, but when he heard Christ's voice: "Francis, go and rebuild my Church, which is falling into ruins," he strove to live the Gospel as best he could. Through God's grace and mercy he rebuilt the Church with the help of the many who joined him. Blessed Teresa of Calcutta was only one woman, but she too said yes to God and made something beautiful of her life for God.

When we say yes to God, we should expect the unexpected. Growing up in New Hampshire, I never expected to walk the streets of Paris one day with a punk rocker from Nebraska, sharing with those we met our faith, hope, and love in Jesus Christ. Over the course of two weeks there, Brother Martin and I spoke with thousands of people and received very different reactions. Some accepted our witness with gratitude, others with indifference, still others with ridicule. We don't know what impact our mission had on these people, but we pray that the Lord will use it to touch many hearts and lead them back to the Way of Life. Jesus sent us to prepare the way for His visit, so that he can reside in their hearts as He does in ours.

Witnessing to and proclaiming the Gospel is more than a duty for

Christ's disciples; it is a joy and privilege. We pray that He will send more laborers into the harvest so that more may come to know His goodness, believe that Jesus is the Savior of the world, and worship God in spirit and truth. Moreover, our hearts rejoice in the Lord, who has looked on His lowly servants with mercy. The Almighty has done great things for us, His weak vessels, and holy is His name. May Jesus Christ be praised now and forever. Amen.

— FR. ANGELUS MARIE HOULE

Father Angelus Marie (left), shown here on a mission in Paris with Brother Martin, reveals how this mission to evangelize is in the very fiber of a friar's being, both priest and lay brother.

Father Bob, one of the founders of our community, is shown giving the call to conversion on Ash Wednesday. He reflects on what "Renewal" in our community's name entails.

"Jesus began to preach, saying, 'Repent, for the kingdom of heaven is at hand.'"

MATTHEW 4:17

CONVERSION / RENEWAL

Some changes are easy to make: changing clothes or hairstyle—or even the TV channels, which we can do without getting off the chair. In our culture we have become accustomed to quick, easy changes without much effort on our part. In the spiritual life, however, change is usually much slower and involves dedication and hard work.

Jesus Christ proclaimed the kingdom of God through reform or conversion of mind and heart. As we know from personal experience, surface changes are easy, but inner change or conversion is much more challenging. That inner transformation is at the heart of Jesus' message to us. We must be uncompromising today in preaching the Gospel. Words alone are not enough: to preach the Gospel effectively, we must have experienced an inner conversion, which is manifested by living out the Gospel message in everyday life.

The Friars and Sisters of the Renewal are dedicated to proclaiming the kingdom through preaching with words and through lives of conversion, striving to live out the teachings of Jesus. We have been blessed with many initiatives to preach the Gospel in parishes and on retreats, using music and drama, as well as words. This blessing extends to daily life as we receive the opportunity to live the Gospel through prayer, community life, and service to the very poor.

God willing, we will give good witness to the Gospel by the way we live together as a community and by our interaction with our neighbors, especially the poor.

— FR. BOB LOMBARDO

*Father Fidelis, shown here, writes from our mission in England
and explains the setting for this picture.*

"And this gospel of the kingdom will be preached throughout the whole world, as a testimony to all nations; and then the end will come."

MATTHEW 24:14

PREACHING

Recently I was preaching during Holy Mass offered in Saint Joseph's Crypt Chapel at Glastonbury, England. This, one of the more ancient Christian sites in England, reputedly founded by Joseph of Arimathea, the man who provided a burial place for our Lord, soon became a major Marian shrine. An old wattle church, dedicated to our Lady, was found on the site when the Saxons arrived at Glastonbury in A.D. 685. A royal charter issued early in the eighth century refers to this church as *ecclesia vetusta beatissimae virginis*, the "old Church of the Most Blessed Virgin," and the "foremost church in Britain, the fount and source of all religion".

As the centuries passed, a great Benedictine monastery rose on the site. It was rebuilt after a fire in 1184, only to be destroyed by a very different attack in the sixteenth century. Following Henry VIII's break with Rome in 1534 over the question of his divorce from Queen Katherine, he proceeded to confiscate Church holdings throughout the country. Glastonbury Abbey was suppressed in 1539, and its last abbot, Richard Whiting, was hanged, drawn, and quartered in November of that year.

The crumbling walls and broken arches of Glastonbury today reflect a far more serious spiritual ruin. The once Catholic town is now a center for the occult, hosting frequent pagan rituals. Its shops offer visitors New Age paraphernalia, the trappings of witchcraft, and unholy objects used for Black Masses.

The light of the Gospel, however, continues to shine in the darkness. The local Catholic Church, across from the abbey ruins, has been the site of annual Eucharist-centered youth retreats emphasizing the presence and mercy of our Lord Jesus. The ancient devotion to our Lady and fidelity to the Catholic Church are growing in the hearts of a new generation of young people as they gather each year at this special shrine.

Neither the devil's malice nor man's infidelity can eclipse the brilliant light of the Gospel of salvation as it is proclaimed to all nations.

— FR. FIDELIS MOSCINSKI

Our love for Pope John Paul was not only because of his sanctity and the great things he did for the world. Similarly, our love for Pope Benedict is not only because of his gifts. Father Andrew, one of our founding friars, shown here receiving a papal blessing as the vice-postulator for the cause of Archbishop Fulton Sheen, writes about this essential component of our reform.

"And he called to him the twelve, and began to send them out two by two, and gave them authority . . ."

MARK 6:7

LOYALTY TO THE HOLY FATHER

Loyalty to the Holy Father was very dear to the heart of Saint Francis of Assisi, who was known to be "truly Catholic and totally apostolic". He impressed this aspect of the charism in the Rule for his friars. In chapter 1, he tells the friars that they are to live the holy Gospel of our Lord; moreover, they are to promise obedience and reverence to the Holy Father and his successors, and they are bound to the Roman Church. In chapter 2, he insists that those who enter the order must "faithfully profess and steadfastly observe the teachings of the Catholic faith and the sacraments of the Church". He ends his Rule by reminding the friars that they are to be "always submissive and subject at the feet of the Holy Roman Church and steadfast in the Catholic faith".

When we began our community in April 1987, our goal was to work "more definitively for personal and communal renewal and for the reform of the Church called for by the Holy Father and many other spiritual leaders since Vatican II". Our constitutions further state that "love for the Church and loyalty to the Holy Father" are among the essential components of this reform. Each friar is expected to have a very deep personal love for the Holy Father, as well as respect for his authority and acceptance of his teachings. It is through the teachings of the Holy Father, joined with a faithful love and loyalty to him, that unity is preserved. The spirit of the Friars of the Renewal is like that of the early Christians who were "of one mind and one heart". The friars find that "unity of mind" by believing the same truths of the Church, and this unity of belief leads to that "unity of heart" in which all work together for God's glory and the building up of the Mystical Body of Christ.

— FR. ANDREW JOSEPH APOSTOLI

Brother John Anthony (top) and Brother Anthony Marie (right) are seen here during hermitage time in upstate New York. Brother Anthony writes of this essential part of the Franciscan life, where the fire of love and devotion is rekindled. One of the places we go for hermitage is Monticello, New York. The name Monticello is literally translated "heavenly mountain". We hope to be transfigured more and more, as Saint Francis was, from these mountaintop times with the Lord.

4. The Transfiguration

"[H]e took with him Peter and John and James, and went up on the mountain to pray. And as he was praying, the appearance of his countenance was altered . . ."

LUKE 9:28–29

HERMITAGE

After having been "changed in mind but not in body," Saint Francis "retired for a short time from the tumult and business of the world and was anxious to keep Jesus Christ in his inmost self." He was accustomed to enter a cave near the city, where he would pray to his heavenly Father in secret. There he consulted God alone about his holy purpose, praying "with all his heart that the eternal and true God guide his way and teach him to do His will."

He endured great suffering of soul, and many thoughts came to disturb him. He repented of his sinful past. When he left the cave, "he was so exhausted from his struggle that one person seemed to have entered, and another to have come out" (Celano's first biography, chap. 3).

Once a month, each friar takes a day or two for what we call hermitage: a period of silent prayer away from our noisy neighborhoods. God can be found in many places, but ultimately, as Elijah experienced, He is in the silent whisper heard in the depths of our hearts.

— BR. ANTHONY MARIE BAETZOLD

Brother Isaac (top) and Brother Juan Diego are shown in moments of prayerful study. Part of the Capuchin tradition that our community inherited is the practice of having two hours of quiet each day for spiritual reading and adoration. Brother Isaac reminds us of the importance of this daily nourishment.

SACRED READING

Thy word is a lamp to my feet and a light to my path. This verse from Psalm 119 aptly describes the power of God's word and our need of its guidance in our lives. True renewal is not a matter of putting our own spin or twist on God's revelation and message so that they suit our needs. Rather, it is a question of allowing this timeless and unchangeable light to shape our interior attitudes and guide us in doing His will and work.

Reading Sacred Scripture prayerfully is an essential aspect of our life, so that His word will light our path and guide our feet in His way. Each morning, the friars have a one-hour period dedicated to spiritual reading and silent prayer, as well as an hour of Eucharistic adoration in the evening. During that time we seek to encounter Jesus Christ in His holy word in Sacred Scripture or other spiritual books.

Saint Francis placed great emphasis on the meditation of God's word. He loved the Gospels and tried to imitate Christ's words and deeds down to the last letter. As Franciscan Friars of the Renewal, seeking to bring Christ to the world, we must be committed to this imitation as well. It was Saint Jerome who said, "Ignorance of Scripture is ignorance of Christ."

During spiritual reading and meditation on God's word we come to a deeper understanding of who Jesus is and who we are. At such times God's word often highlights our sinfulness, weakness, and need for healing. This is not a comfortable experience; sometimes an encounter with truth in the Gospels is like being spiritually mugged. But self-knowledge is necessary to lead us to repentance and greater reliance on Jesus.

Thomas Merton once wrote that after his reading from Sacred Scripture, the trees looked more green and full, the sky seemed a deeper blue, and life was richer and more full. This is often our experience. Sacred reading—encountering God's holy word—puts life in perspective and reminds us why we are here, why we are doing what we are doing, and Who indeed has called us here to do His work.

Without the light of God's word to shape our lives we would cease to be Friars of the Renewal, and our work would lose its value. Truly, His word is a lamp unto our feet and a light unto our path.

— BR. ISAAC MARY SPINHARNEY

Brother Leopold is shown using his gift of woodcarving, and Brother Nathaniel is tending the garden at Saint Crispin's Friary, an oasis of beauty in the neighborhood. Brother Ephrem (right), our main tailor, is cutting material for a habit. Brother Leopold reflects on the transfiguration of material goods to reveal God's glory.

CONTEMPLATIVE LABOR

Beauty, in one of its facets, may be seen as God's love materially expressed. In the Book of Genesis, God saw that everything He created was good. All of creation reflects His goodness and beauty. The human person, therefore, being made in the image and likeness of God, also reflects His beauty, goodness, and love. God became man, and in His humanity shone forth the highest beauty of creation. Yet what was seen at the Transfiguration was barely a shadow of what is to come.

In Christ's Transfiguration the apostles caught a glimpse of divine love, which was veiled in Christ's humanity and even now remains hidden in the Eucharist. Man, who is made in God's image, is called to create, to draw order out of the disorder that comes through original sin. Art portrays the beauty within. Yet even what is most ugly, manifested in the Crucifixion, becomes beautiful through Christ's love "portraying" our salvation.

Man is called to transfigure the world into beauty. Manual labor and art go hand in hand, as man participates in God's creation. We create with God when we garden, sew, or sculpt, and what we achieve is but a rude image of the beauty and order that God originally bestowed on the world. Our cooperation with the work of creation is a childlike imitation of God the Father, who created everything, but we thus participate in the transfiguration of the world so that His kingdom may come on earth as it is in heaven.

— Br. Leopold Mariae Bokulich

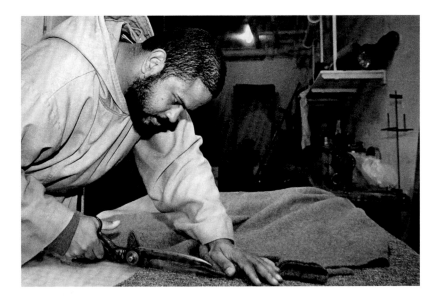

More than anything else in his writings, Saint Francis emphasized the reverence we should have for the Body and Blood of the Lord. Brother Augustine Mary, here at his duties as a sacristan, explains.

5. *The Eucharist*

"Jesus sent Peter and John, saying, 'Go and prepare the passover for us, that we may eat it.'"

LUKE 22:8

THE SACRISTY—
PREPARING THE UPPER ROOM

The Eucharist is "the source and summit of the Christian life" (*Lumen Gentium*, no. 11). That is an incredible statement and easily said, but not necessarily understood. It means that the Eucharist is everything to us! It means that the holy Sacrifice of the Mass, and our partaking in the Body and Blood of our Lord, is the most important event in our lives. That is, there is nothing in the whole world that can substitute or supercede its primacy. For, in the Eucharist we discover our salvation and that for which we exist, namely, Jesus.

Therefore, it is because of our faith in and love for the Eucharist that the sacristan pays such attention to the preparation of the divine liturgy. Everything he touches in the sacristy has a sacred purpose. The chalice he shines so carefully, for example, is the vessel that will hold the most precious Blood of our Lord, the Blood shed for the salvation of the world. The stoles and other of the priest's vestments are also carefully prepared because they will be worn by those who stand *in persona Christi*, that is, by those who are mysteriously and sacramentally other Christs and who alone are capable of offering the pure and unblemished sacrifice.

For these reasons the sacristan has an awesome responsibility. His is a humble, hidden work that often goes unnoticed. But like so many things that seem insignificant, his work becomes, in the shadow of the Holy One, divine.

— BR. AUGUSTINE MARY CONNER

Father Conrad is shown distributing the Body and Blood of Christ at a pilgrimage Mass.
Father Fidelis is bringing Jesus to young people at a Eucharistic procession during a Youth 2000 retreat.
These retreats allow young people to experience the powerful presence of Christ in a personal way in the Eucharist.
Father Conrad shares his thoughts with us.

"Do this in remembrance of me."

LUKE 22:19

BRINGING CHRIST TO OTHERS IN COMMUNION

I experience a solidarity with the world through the Body and Blood of Jesus when I receive Him at Mass each morning. Our Lord's institution of the Eucharist as the sacramental expression of His life, death, and Resurrection is indeed a mystery of light. Pope John Paul II has best expressed what I want to say: "The Eucharist should have a power to transform beyond Sunday Mass and into daily life."

My life as a Franciscan Friar of the Renewal is punctuated by prayer. The Eucharist is the greatest prayer of the day. From morning Mass until the evening Holy Hour before the Blessed Sacrament, there is grace flowing so that I can live in solidarity with those all around me.

Through Jesus in the Eucharist I unite myself in solidarity with the needs of our poor neighbors. The day's work will include reaching out to them with some charitable help. I am united to the need for world peace and the need for a new evangelization in our time. I am joined to the greatest need of our time: to protect the dignity of all human life from conception to natural death.

God gives Himself each day in His sacred word and in His Body and Blood. In the Eucharist I am drawn to Christ to pray, work, and be offered for others with Jesus Christ.

— FR. CONRAD OSTERHOUT

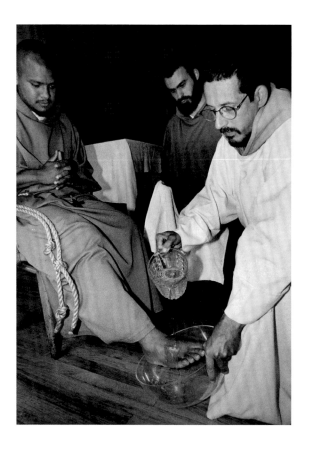

Father Glenn, one of our founding friars, has been our Community Servant (Superior).
He is shown in a liturgical moment of washing feet and in a more common moment
of service. He tells us what Franciscan leadership is meant to be.

SERVING THE COMMUNITY

In a series of writings known as the Admonitions, Saint Francis included this counsel to the friars: "Those who are put in charge of others should be no prouder of their office than if they had been appointed to wash the feet of their brothers. They should be no more upset at the loss of their authority than they would be if they were deprived of the task of washing feet. The more they are upset, the greater the risk they incur to their souls." I suspect Saint Francis wrote this because a friar might be reluctant to relinquish his position of authority in the brotherhood. The Saint's well-aimed admonition certainly must have loosened the grip of any friar who was holding on to the helm just a bit too tightly.

It is of interest that Saint Francis named his fraternity the Friars Minor, or the Lesser Brothers. Humility and fraternal charity were to be the hallmarks of this religious family. Therefore, he desired that those friars assigned or elected to office not be called superiors, but rather *minister*, a Latin word meaning "servant". In another Admonition he wrote: "The ministers should receive them [the friars] charitably and kindly, and show such familiarity that these same friars may speak with them and treat them as masters with their servants, for so it ought to be that the ministers should be the servant of the friars."

I thank God that for the past six years I have had the privilege of serving the friars as the Community Servant. People often ask me if the responsibility of being the superior is difficult. I tell them: "When I think and act like a superior, my position is a burden; yet when I remember that I'm a servant, it becomes a blessing!"

In the Gospels, our Lord teaches us that a true disciple follows Him in word and deed. Therefore, if Christ came down from heaven and bowed down to wash the feet of His disciples, shouldn't His disciples do the same? To have any authority over others means we must be sensitive to the needs of those entrusted to us and humbly bend low to serve, even to wash their feet.

If we did this for one another, life and labor would cease being a burden and become what God intended them to be—a blessing!

— Fr. Glenn Sudano

III

THE SORROWFUL MYSTERIES

*Brother Felix Mary (seated) and Father Herald are shown keeping watch with a woman in Honduras
in her last moments of earthly life. Franciscans are called to the active-contemplative life,
and prayer is the great gift we have to offer.
Brother Felix reminds us to persevere in prayer.*

1. *The Agony in the Garden*

"Then he said to them, 'My soul is very sorrowful, even to death; remain here, and watch with me.'"

MATTHEW 26:38

PRAYER

If we are to be true sons of Saint Francis, we must strive to be authentic men of prayer, a goal that must be at the very heart of our life. There are many forms of prayer, one of which is contemplation.

"Wait here. . . . Watch and pray." So Jesus said to Peter, James, and John at Gethsemane, just before He was to suffer His Passion and death. Watch. Look at Jesus. Fix your gaze on Him. See Him in the garden, agonizing to embrace His Father's will. See Him scourged, mocked, and crucified for love of us.

See Him heal the sick, raise the dead, and forgive sinners. See Him instruct the crowds, multiply the loaves and fish, and calm the violent storm. See Him in the Eucharist, waiting for us in silence, in meekness and humility, in patience and frailty. See Him. Watch Him.

Saint John Marie Vianney, the Curé of Ars, once asked an old man in his parish how he could spend so much time in church. "What do you do there?" The answer was simple: "I look at the good God, and He looks at me." Look, then, at Jesus. He is waiting for you.

Jesus also told the apostles to wait for Him. At times we can no longer "see" the Lord. He seems to be absent. We are His servants, however, and it is our duty to wait on the Master of the household. He may leave by a door through which we cannot pass. In that case we must continue to wait for Him, keeping our eyes on that door. Perhaps He will return and invite us to enter by the same door, enter more deeply into Him.

Look at the good God, because He is always looking at you.

— BR. FELIX MARY DESILETS

The meaning of renewal is experienced in the most profound way in the sacrament of Penance, as Father Mariusz Casimir, pictured here, writes.

Father Raphael Jacques, shown here at the front of a pilgrimage in Pennsylvania, came to our community as a diocesan priest from France. He adds his witness to this amazing sacrament.

2. The Scourging at the Pillar

"[U]pon him was the chastisement that made us whole, and with his stripes we are healed."

ISAIAH 53:5

CONFESSION

The crucified Lord fulfills the purpose of the Incarnation as the Lamb of God who came to take away the sins of the world. Christ became sin in order to free us from this slavery to death, to die on our behalf, to give us life. Therefore, forgiveness by our God is not cheaply come by. Forgiveness comes from the precious suffering and death of Jesus on the Cross: "Father, forgive them . . ." The Blood of Christ makes us clean!

To be a priest *in persona Christi* is well expressed in the forgiveness of the sacrament of Penance: "I absolve you . . ." In his apostolic exhortation *On Reconciliation and Penance* (1984), Pope John Paul II reminds us that the priest acts in the sacrament of Penance in the person of Christ, in whose name he absolves the sinner. He wrote, "This is undoubtedly the most difficult and sensitive, the most exhausting and demanding ministry of the priest, but also one of the most beautiful and consoling" (no. 29).

To renew the Church, it is essential to restore a love for the sacrament in which the Blood of Christ can wash us clean.

— Fr. Mariusz Casimir Koch

I have been a priest for twenty years now, and the Eucharist is the center of my life. But I always say with the same emotion, as at my first Mass, "This is my body. . . This is my blood . . . Do this in memory of me."

Since I joined the Friars of the Renewal, I have discovered another aspect of my vocation, namely, to testify to the mercy and love of God. Recently I heard the confessions of several men and women who came back to the Church after an absence of ten, twenty, thirty, and even forty years. The priest has an amazing power—which is first of all a duty—to welcome those "who were lost and have been found." I feel that at last I am living the fulfillment of my priesthood in accord with my religious name, Raphael, which in Hebrew signifies "medicine of God".

— Fr. Raphael Jacques Chilou

Brother Matteo is shown here visiting a family in the friars' neighborhood (and helping an intrigued girl cut her fingernails). Father Herald Joseph, the local Servant of the friary, gives us a view into the distressing disguise of Jesus in our Honduran neighbors.

3. The Crowning with Thorns

"He was despised and rejected by men; a man of sorrows, and
acquainted with grief."

ISAIAH 53:3

MISSION—HONDURAS

There's something unusual about being a missionary in an already
Catholic country. The first Mass offered in the Americas was said in
1502 in what is now northern Honduras, and the country's long Christian
history is often overlooked or even exploited unknowingly by Evangelical
Christians.

Central America, particularly Honduras and Nicaragua, has lagged far
behind North and South America in social and religious development.
Poverty here is extreme, and the infrastructure is tenuous. The Church
struggles to stay on her feet. Even now, five hundred years after the first
Mass was said in Honduras, there are fewer than 200 native Honduran
priests.

Christ has come to Honduras, but He has not yet come to full stature
(see Ephesians 4:13). Therefore, we labor side by side with our Honduran
brothers and sisters—priests, laity, and religious—to build up the Body of
Christ through evangelization, catechesis, formation, and growth in holiness. We have also carried out a number of *Pan de vida* Eucharistic
retreats for young people, as well as Eucharistic missions in mountain
village chapels, where often the Blessed Sacrament has never been re-
served or exposed for adoration and where Mass may be celebrated only
a few times a year. We assist in celebrating the sacraments in local
parishes, religious communities, and institutions. We have had the privilege and blessing of collaborating with a lay Catholic group, the
Missioners of Christ, in engaging in public evangelization activities in
parks and going door to door with the message of the Gospel and the
Catholic faith. With the same group we have also conducted programs
for children and young people.

Christ has come to Honduras, but He has yet to rise from the dead
here. The country lives in a kind of perpetual, enforced Lent. Many
penitential practices, freely undertaken by our community and by other
Catholics at specific times, are obligatory and unending here because of
the extreme poverty. Most Hondurans endure fasting and abstinence because of their restricted diet of rice, beans, and tortillas. Meat, milk, and

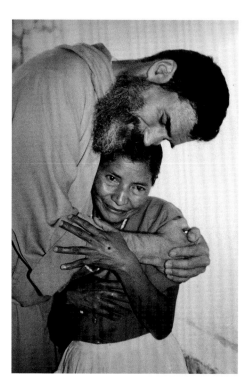

HONDURAS MISSION:
*Father Terry comforts a homeless woman in distress
and speaks a word of encouragement to some farmers in the mountains.*

fresh vegetables are a luxury. Many sleep on cold dirt floors; mattresses and warm clothes are hard to come by. Often entire families share a single towel and sleep in the same bed. Access to electricity is a step above the norm, and indoor plumbing is an enviable rarity. Basic survival, which includes cutting firewood and hauling water, is a lot of work. Medical needs and health conditions that would be easily treated in a developed country exist in epidemic proportions here, and not infrequently result in death.

Our response to this ongoing state of emergency is not highly developed social action programs but rather the simple remedy of the Gospel: feeding the hungry, giving drink to the thirsty, clothing the naked, sheltering the homeless, and caring for the sick. Put more biblically: we feed Jesus who was hungry in the desert and give drink to Him who cried, "I thirst." We clothe Christ who was stripped of His garments and shelter Him who had "no place to lay His head". We visit Jesus who was arrested and held prisoner, seeing and touching the wounds in His body.

Working with Light of the World charities, we carry out medical missions and have constructed a small health clinic and surgical center for the poor, which is named for the eighteenth-century homeless beggar Saint Benedict Joseph Labré. At Casa Guadalupe, a neighborhood center we built next to our friary, we conduct much of our apostolic efforts to evangelize and serve the poor.

The giving has not been a one-way street. Our experience has been an exchange of spiritual gifts. Living in Honduras has enabled us to experience essential elements of Christianity that are elusive in developed nations. Responding to the needs of the poor is indispensable for a Christian, an essential part of preaching and living the Gospel. It is also an invitation to experience Christ's presence and the reality of His kingdom among the poor and to see certain Gospel scenes come to life. As Father Benedict observed during a recent visit to the mission: "This is the world of the New Testament." We would like to share this grace with mission visitors who come to stay at Casa Guadalupe.

Honduras is at a crossroads. While it is still a Catholic country and the majority of the people are baptized Catholics, that reality is threatened. Spiritual fragmentation is undermining the foundation of common faith that has unified Honduran culture since the colonial era. The country is now increasingly defenseless against the pervasive threat of secularism, which is propagated through the mass media.

HONDURAS MISSION:
The girl wearing a rosary around her neck is an emblem of the hope—and the struggles—present in the Honduras mission.

Saint Seraphim Friary is shown above.

Perhaps the presence of the Friars of the Renewal in Honduras, even though they are struggling to get a foothold, will help to preserve the spiritual treasure and heritage of this beautiful country and people.

— Fr. Herald Joseph Brock

HONDURAS MISSION:
*The young people of all ages do their part to help the friars
with regular food distribution to local families.*

The crown of thorns our Savior wore was transformed into a crown of glory.
Brother Agostino Miguel, shown here, shares a glimpse of this glory as witnessed in our Honduran mission.

MISSION—HONDURAS

One day, I visited a poor single mother who was ill and who lived down the road from our friary. Although she had had acute abdominal pain, she knew she had to work to provide for her family. When she was no longer able to work, she went to the hospital and we got word of her illness. She said something to me that was very profound: "The poor man is happy as long as his health is good. As long as they have their food and shelter, they can get by, but when his health is bad, he has nothing." Her eyes were sad, but her resolve was true; and happily, she recovered from her illness. I looked at her children, and I knew some of what they had suffered, but the room was filled with smiles.

All the people we visited in the slums and mountain villages of Honduras had this in common. There was always a happiness that touched your heart. While we were there to bring the Good News and they were happy to receive it, they too transmitted the Gospel through their lives in the daily tragedy that surrounded them.

Some of the homes we visited had next to nothing, yet they possessed a treasure that eludes most of the world's happiness. Some remote mountain villages took us back to the days before electricity, telephones, and television. The people ate what they had sown and reaped, and they shared their meager food with us. They also shared their joy of life, which I still carry in my heart and which is a life-giving memory. It is also an example of the strength of the human spirit, which those with nothing have in such abundance.

— Br. Agostino Miguel Torres

Brother Damiano (top), who has a background in nursing,
is taking care of a young patient at our free clinic in the South Bronx.
Sister Clare Marie and Father Thomas help an older man from the Bronx.
As Saint Francis found Jesus in the lepers living so close to him, Sister Clare Marie
reminds us that we don't have to go far to find Him in His distressing disguise.

SERVICE TO THE POOR

One of my early memories, perhaps even my earliest, is of my father at my bedside, leading me in my bedtime prayers, which were always addressed to "our heavenly Father". They always contained the petition that He help us "not take our many gifts for granted".

Even though I surely did (and do) take the abundant gifts of our good God for granted, I grew up with an awareness of both God's loving Providence and the world's poor. A desire grew and settled in me to become a missionary, to live a life of helping the poor and needy.

As a child, I pictured myself in an obscure African or South American village; but as I grew a bit older, I recognized that I need not travel far to find God's beloved poor. The United States has plenty of its own people with none (or little) of what it takes to have an average or decent life. Perhaps worse are the terrible isolation and loneliness that so many people feel.

The need for a smile, a hand, or a listening ear is as great as, if not greater than, any material need. As a Christian and a Franciscan, I see these small services and acts of love as extensions of my faith. With the eyes of faith, I see Jesus, and I know that whatever we do for the least of His brothers and sisters, we have done for Him.

— Sr. Clare Marie Matthiass

*Brother Jacob (top) lends an ear to a homeless man in Manhattan,
and Brother Shawn Conrad serves dinner at Saint Padre Pio Shelter.
Brother Shawn reminds us that our service to the poor goes much deeper than
material provisions and "social work".*

SERVICE TO THE POOR

The works of mercy, both corporal and spiritual, play an essential role in any Christian life, and for the Franciscan it is an even greater responsibility. From the very beginning, the Friars of the Renewal have attempted to live out the works of mercy in a concrete way. Every night of the year, since December 2, 1987, Saint Padre Pio Shelter has opened its doors to homeless men. A warm bed and a hot meal are provided for each one, in a setting that is far more like a home than a shelter. There is an opportunity to relax in a peaceful atmosphere far removed from the cruelty of street life.

Besides satisfying material needs and creature comforts, the friars and sisters, along with many dedicated volunteers who staff the shelter, have the privilege of helping the men get back things that are their rights by birth: dignity and self-respect. In the face of each man who walks through the door we strive to see the face of Jesus and treat him as if he were Christ Himself. This is our opportunity to put flesh to the words of Jesus: "[A]s you did it to one of the least of these my brethren, you did it to me" (Matthew 25:40).

— Br. Shawn Conrad

Father Sylvester reflects on the grateful devotion to Christ crucified
that Catholics express, particularly on Good Friday.

4. Jesus Carries His Cross

"If any man would come after me, let him deny himself and take up his cross daily and follow me."

LUKE 9:23

LOVE OF THE CROSS

Seeing Sister Lucille kiss the Cross made me wonder how people usually conjure up warm and wonderful images of a birdbath when they think of Saint Francis: Francis with his feathered friends fluttering about. Granted, Francis did preach to larks occasionally. But he was not about a birdbath; rather he was about a bloodbath—a saving stream flowing from the Savior's pierced side. What burning love must have surged in the heart of this saint as he contemplated the Cross of Christ!

One of the more ancient and beloved traditions in the Church is devotion to the Cross of Christ. As early as the fourth century, the Church Fathers tell us, pilgrims went to Jerusalem to venerate the true Cross, "on which hung the Savior of the world". We Franciscans, in the spirit of our founding father, especially revere the mysterious events of Good Friday.

Saint Francis is the example par excellence of love for and devotion to the Crucified. Indeed, the Saint's whole life could be considered a living *via crucis*, or Way of the Cross. Beginning in the little dilapidated chapel of San Damiano as he gazed on the crucifix, he heard Jesus say to him, "Francis, repair my house. . . ." He immediately began to restore little churches, but he soon recognized that the call to renewal had deeper implications for the Church and himself. He took up his cross, namely, the Franciscan habit, which is cruciform.

Meanwhile God's grace was renewing Saint Francis interiorly. He began to see the face of his crucified Savior in all who suffered, and his love moved him to action. Like Simon of Cyrene, he helped the poorest of the poor carry their crosses. Like Veronica, he wiped the face of Jesus in the lepers. Like the women of Jerusalem who wept for love of Him, Francis wept, exclaiming, "Love is not loved." He became so spiritually crucified that he made up in himself "what is lacking in Christ's afflictions" (see Colossians 1:24). As Francis neared the end of his *via crucis*, the Savior set His seal on his flesh while the saint was contemplating the triumph of the Cross. This miraculous sign—the stigmata—unveils the depths of Saint Francis's love for the Cross.

Indeed, Saint Francis, bathed in Christ's blood, stands as a living icon of the crucified Savior. The larks have flown away long ago. But men and women seeking to be renewed in Christ still flock to the Poor Man of Assisi, and he shows them how to walk the noble way of the Cross.

— Fr. Sylvester Mary Mann

WITNESSES OF THE CROSS

Every year on Good Friday, we pray the Stations of the Cross as a short pilgrimage through the streets of Harlem and the Bronx. The brothers take turns carrying the Cross and wearing a crown of thorns. As I soon realized, it is not only a humiliating experience but also it hurts! The wooden cross is heavy, and the thorns prick.

It is easy to say that Jesus came to bring us new life, but the font that pours new life into our souls is the Passion and death of Jesus. If we take up our cross and die to ourselves in the way Jesus taught us, we might through His grace merit everlasting life in the Resurrection. Instead, we generally fast-forward to the Resurrection scene.

In an attempt to remind ourselves of the need to carry our figurative cross, we literally take up a cross. We also hope to remind others of Christ's salvific way by bringing the Cross to them in their daily lives on the streets. Some people laugh, some people stare, others cover their mouths in shock. Some people take the opportunity to recognize the meaning of the Cross. Others, convinced that they have already seen it all, walk briskly past, hardly noticing. Our hope is that through us Christ will encounter some person in need of grace.

Brothers, sisters, and lay friends follow behind the procession, handing out Bibles and rosaries, and talking with people. God does the work. We just try to open doors for Him.

— Br. Bonaventure Mary Rummell

Father Benedict (top) is shown preaching at the Missionaries of Charity convent in the Bronx.

Brother John Bosco (middle) and Brother Bonaventure Mary (bottom) take their turn carrying the Cross in a Good Friday procession.

We annually commemorate Good Friday and other major liturgical days in the street, as well as in a church. Brother Bonaventure explains.

PILGRIMAGE

Our life here on earth is a pilgrimage. The Church is often referred to as the "pilgrim" Church because it "'will receive its perfection only in the glory of heaven (LG 48),' at the time of Christ's glorious return. Until that day, 'the Church progresses on her pilgrimage amidst this world's persecutions and God's consolations (Saint Augustine, *De civ. Dei*, 18, 51)'" (*Catechism of the Catholic Church*, no. 769).

Therefore, as Christians we are pilgrims. We are merely passing through this world, awaiting our true homeland in heaven. On this particular four-day pilgrimage, known as the Polish pilgrimage, many priests, religious brothers and sisters, married couples, single men and women, and children gather for a sixty-mile walk that begins in Great Meadows, New Jersey, and ends at Our Lady of Czestochowa shrine in Doylestown, Pennsylvania. During the pilgrimage we not only walk, but pray, rest, sing, and eat together, as we attempt to witness to the mercy and love of God and the truths of our Catholic faith in a world that desperately needs it.

Like daily life, the Polish pilgrimage is filled with many challenges, yet "the victory that overcomes the world" is our faith (see 1 John 5:4). By God's grace we all survive, and continue to proclaim that victory in the events of daily life, as we strive to grow in holiness while we are still on our earthly pilgrimage.

— Br. Jeremiah Myriam Shryock

Brother Sharbel Mariam finds a creative way to lift high the Cross for the pilgrims (top left).

Brothers Emmanuel and Gabriel, along with Brothers Leopold and John Anthony, take a moment for restful prayer along the way (top right).

And Father Joseph Mary joins in song with the pilgrims.

Brother Jeremiah Myriam introduces us to the Polish pilgrimage.

Up to this point, none of the friars of our community have passed away.
This photo shows a scene from a religious play, which is enacted each year on the eve of Saint Francis's feast,
when Franciscans commemorate his death, or passage to heaven, known in the Order as the transitus.
Brother Philip Maria Allen, who portrayed Saint Francis, writes of his role in the ceremony.

5. *The Crucifixion and Death of Jesus*

"If any man would come after me, let him deny himself and take up
his cross daily and follow me."

LUKE 9:23

THE "TRANSITUS"

I was profoundly blessed not only to act a role but almost to become Saint Francis and enter his mind, heart, and life. I listened and prayed intently during the production, as the narrator read authentic Franciscan texts. I journeyed through the youth, conversion, prayer, life, and death of this remarkable man. In one scene, I was following the mystical experience of receiving the stigmata—the impression of the five wounds of our crucified Savior—in my hands, feet, and side. I was moved almost to tears when the brothers carried me, as the dead Francis, through the Church on their shoulders. Blind and racked with pain, the seraphic saint had died while singing of divine love.

After my experience at the *transitus*, Saint Francis became utterly real to me, a faithful friend and mighty intercessor in heaven! I pray that he will intercede for you to receive the grace to become, in imitation of Christ, truly humble in mind and heart, poor in fact and in spirit, and charitable in thought, word, and deed.

— BR. PHILIP MARIA ALLEN

Father Luke, the vocational director for our community, is seen here professing his final vows.
Our consecration relates us to many mysteries in the life of Christ, particularly to this one, as he explains.

"Then Jesus, crying with a loud voice, said, 'Father, into thy hands I commit my spirit!'"

LUKE 23:46

THE MYSTERY OF SELF-OFFERING

The beginning of Jesus' agony in the garden of Gethsemane began with His free entrustment: "Father, . . . not my will, but yours, be done." His sufferings were completed with the cry, "Father, into your hands I commit my spirit!" (Luke 22:42; 23:46). Indeed, "Greater love has no man than this, that a man lay down his life for his friends" (John 15:13). Because Jesus, the Christ, is God, we are to understand that His life was not so much taken from Him but freely given by Him. See how the Cross stands revealed as the tree of life!

Christianity is a religion of martyrdom. The self-offering love of the Crucifixion displays a power that unties the knot of suicide bombings and abortion. Yet Jesus did not suffer and die on the Cross in order that we not have to suffer and die. Rather, He suffered and died so that we *can* suffer and die *with great purpose and peace*. We consecrate our own suffering and dying by uniting them with the sufferings and death of Jesus. The evangelical counsels, or three vows, that all Catholic religious make are a reply to the invitation from Jesus: "Follow me."

June 10, 2001, my classmates and I professed final vows of poverty, chastity, and obedience. During my solitude retreat before profession, I recalled the years of discernment, doubt, hope, and prayer, all of which had prepared the way for what I was about to do. I had found God's will for my life, His plan for me. From that moment, my life has become a living prayer: "Thy kingdom come, thy will be done". Embracing the mystery of the Cross, I freely entrusted the sacrifice of my life, with Jesus, into our Father's hands.

Every night at Compline, we chant the same prayer of entrustment that Jesus spoke from the Cross. It completed His prayer in the garden, and it completes our day. While praying these profound words, I always fix my eyes on the pierced hands of Jesus on the crucifix. Truly, our lives are in His hands. Like little children holding their father's hand while crossing the street, let us trust Him in all things and live our lives for God.

— FR. LUKE MARY FLETCHER

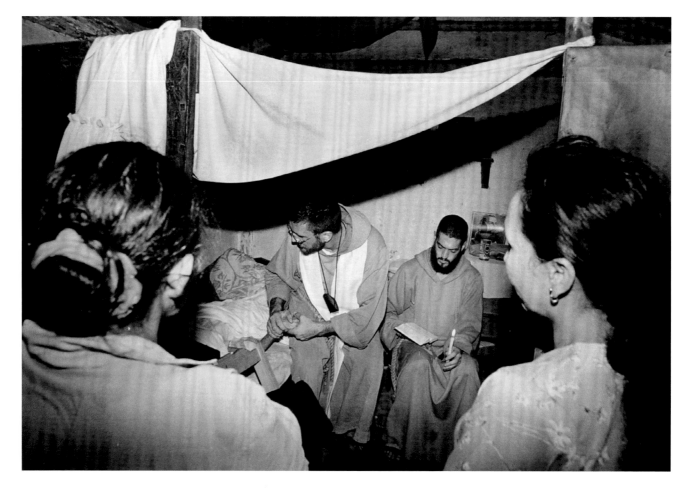

Father Herald Joseph (left) and Brother Felix kept vigil with this woman until her soul passed "beyond the veil".
Franciscan preachers throughout the ages have awakened Christians to the priority of the spiritual life with two simple words:
"remember death". The friars in Honduras are often reminded of this wisdom, as Father Herald tells us.

"And when the centurion, who stood facing him, saw that he thus breathed his last, he said, 'Truly this man was the Son of God!'"

MARK 15:39

DYING

What a terrifying privilege to be with someone in the last moments of this life and help him to prepare to pass through the portal of death into eternal life. This is an almost weekly experience for us in Honduras, where doctors, hospitals, and priests are few, life is short, and death is never far away. Sometimes we even have an extra coffin on hand in our friary—just in case.

Our regular encounters with death are like being doused with ice-cold water: they keep us spiritually awake, alert, and vigilant. "We should have a daily familiarity with death", writes Saint Ambrose, reflecting on the death of his brother Satyrus, in a passage we read each year on All Souls' Day. It is in the face of death that, somehow, life's meaning emerges more clearly.

Yet it is not only in the face of death that life's meaning becomes clear; because, by itself, death remains a crushing, answerless enigma. Something is necessary: the gift of the Cross. The Cross holds the key that unlocks the mystery of suffering and death. It is a beacon that shines with the bright light of hope in the dark valley of human despair; it is the staff on which we lean for strength when the weight of sorrow is too heavy to bear. It is not simply that we carry the Cross; the Cross carries us, too.

— FR. HERALD JOSEPH BROCK

IV

THE GLORIOUS MYSTERIES

1. The Resurrection

"I came that they may have life, and have it abundantly."

JOHN 10:10

FREEDOM

In the *Little Flowers of Saint Francis*—a collection of short stories of the saint's early life—there is an account of his spinning one of the brothers around one day, causing the friar to fall down in dizziness. In the story, Saint Francis decided that the friars would continue their journey in the direction toward which the brother fell.

It is a great joy to be a Franciscan friar or sister and to have the freedom to jump into many adventures in the Catholic Church. Adventures abound in religious life—the sacraments, prayer, retreats, pilgrimages, giving talks, and much else. I love to meet young people where they are in life, whether on the basketball court or the playing field, and lead them (I hope) from a playful to a prayerful experience. How can others learn to trust us if we do not spend time with them? How can we get to know someone? When the apostles asked Jesus where He was staying, he answered, "Come and see." The simple joy of living is contagious!

If you visit one of our friaries, you will experience the joy of the adventure, as we trust in Jesus because He is with us, as He promised, every step, every jump of the way!

— BR. SIMON MARIE DANKOSKI

Brother Simon (top), Brother Pio (middle)—and Brother Isaac, Brother Augustine, and Father Juniper—show that youth springs eternal in the friars.

Our witness would not be convincing, worthwhile, or joyful if it wasn't also stamped with the Resurrection victory of our Redeemer. The hope of the Resurrection assures us that we need not be afraid, nor should we take ourselves too seriously. Brother Simon Marie helps us to make this leap of faith.

We took it as a sign from the Lord that a number of men came from England, wishing to join our community; it meant that we should open a friary there. Brother John Paul, shown here, writes from our first friary outside New York.

2. The Ascension

"[Y]ou shall be my witnesses . . . to the end of the earth."

ACTS 1:8

MISSION (ENGLAND)

Franciscan friars first set foot on English soil in 1224. Saint Francis had sent a deacon named Agnellus of Pisa and eight other friars on a mission. When the boat carrying them arrived at Dover, they were suspected of being thieves and were threatened with hanging, but their openness and joyful humor saved them that first day. Within a week, they had reached Canterbury, where they were housed in a small room behind the school hall. Part of their ancient dwelling still exists in Canterbury, despite the destruction of religious houses in England in the sixteenth century. In England, the term "Greyfriars" refers to Franciscans because of the grayish color of their undyed woolen habits.

On Ascension Thursday, 2000, four Friars of the Renewal, including me, were sent to open our first mission friary in England. We arrived in a country with far fewer Catholics than there had been in the thirteenth century, and we were greeted with both hospitality and hostility as we moved into London's East End. Christ's Presence came into our friary shortly after our arrival, when a Mass of thanksgiving was offered. His Presence and our dual witness of evangelization and work with the poor have provided many opportunities to share the Gospel, as they did with the first Franciscan friars who came to England nearly eight hundred years earlier. We hope to open a second friary in England soon.

In an address to the bishops of England and Wales, Pope John Paul II made a special appeal to religious to renew their commitment to serve also in poorer areas. He went on to say, "In places where much exists to lure youth away from the path of truth and genuine freedom, the consecrated person's witness to the evangelical counsels is an irreplaceable gift."

— BR. JOHN PAUL OUELLETTE

WITNESS

Saint Francis enthusiastically told his friars, "The world is our cloister." In others words, a friar is a monk on the move, a mobile monk. I am amazed at the number of places our work of evangelization takes us to, causing us sometimes to be called the "Frequent Flyers of the Renewal".

Time spent in planes, trains, and automobiles is not time wasted; rather it becomes part of the fabric of our life of prayer and witness. Many Christians would probably agree that the subway lends itself to prayer, not only because of its general etiquette of quiet, but also because each train car usually contains a microcosm of the world's inhabitants and reminds us of the solidarity and intercessory prayer to which we are called. Driving in New York lends itself to prayer for many obvious reasons (as with the story of the taxi driver whose reward was great in heaven for getting so many of his customers to pray—out of fear for their lives!). The brothers have noticed that praying the Rosary seems to make traffic jams dissipate more quickly, or at least the frustration behind the wheel!

As we converse with the Lord along the world's highways, He also puts all kinds of people in our path for us to listen and witness to. Little children in airports and city streets often exclaim, "Mommy, look. It's God," or "It's Jesus." My own favorite is, "Hi, Church!" Older folks sometimes say, "God bless you", and smile.

On the other hand, some people snicker when they see us and roll their eyes or elbow their friend in the side. As we stepped onto a train in London, a man said to us, "Don't try to convert me; I'm a pagan." Those who respond negatively are particularly "targeted" by us for conversation or at least for prayer. Meeting them seems as important as getting to wherever we are going.

Especially memorable are those who ask for prayers and quickly open their hearts between three stops on the subway. Sometimes my last word in these brief encounters is, "If I don't see you again in this life, I look forward to seeing you in heaven and catching up on all that the Lord did for you." As we walk along the busy sidewalk, we pray that the strangers around us will make it to heaven. Part of the revelation of God's glory and goodness will be hearing from each person how the Lord managed to get them there.

That, of course, is the most important trip of all.

— Fr. Richard Roemer

Father Richard (opposite) in a quiet moment on the subway in New York, while Brother Albert (above) sings on a subway in Toronto during the World Youth Day.

Consecrated life includes being a public witness of the kingdom of heaven, as Father Richard writes.

Father Juniper (left) and Father Thomas are shown passing out palm branches in the Bronx on Palm Sunday. Brother John Bosco reminds us that, in imitating Christ, we are to bring the Good News to the poor.

WITNESS

How is it that in the most crime-ridden areas of the city, where drug addiction, prostitution, and gang violence are commonplace, people respect the Cross of Jesus and those who wear the habit? Yet in the more respectable neighborhoods of downtown, New York people are indifferent.

One day, when I was riding the number 19 bus between the Bronx and Harlem, a woman came and sat next to me. She said she had been compelled to come over and speak with me. With tears streaming from her eyes, she related how she was feeling intense anger and hatred toward a company that had dealt with her deceased mother's apartment. She even spoke of physical revenge. I listened to her and then spoke to her about the need for forgiveness and God's love. She thanked me warmly and got off the bus.

Encounters like this are commonplace in the city. The light of Jesus shines through the poor, not only in their brokenness and humility, but also in their honesty and thirst for recognition.

— Br. John Bosco Mills

Perhaps the most evident sign of the presence of the Holy Spirit
is unity among diverse personalities and backgrounds.
Here, Brother Michael observes Father Benedict at work (above);
and Father Juniper (left) discusses the Scriptures with Brother Gabriel.
Brother Michael reflects on the personal and relational emphases of our lives.

3. *The Descent of the Holy Spirit*

"Now there are varieties of gifts, but the same Spirit . . ."

I CORINTHIANS 12:4

FRATERNAL LIFE

We have a saying in our community—that some aspects of our vocation cannot be taught; they must be caught. Most, if not all, of this "catching" occurs in relationships. Our first relationship is with our Lord Jesus, which sets us within the dynamic relationship of the Most Holy Trinity. Franciscans must also have a relationship with our holy father Saint Francis, whose life inspires us to live the Gospel with a particular devotion to Lady Poverty. We must also have a deep relationship with one another. The brothers can be a joy for us—and at times can cause us difficulties. Our communal life is lived in an intense environment; our prayers, both personal and communal, pull us out of ourselves and put us at the service of the needs of the greater Church.

Our evening examination of faults prods us to self-knowledge and correction. Knowing our own faults and those of the other brothers is humbling. In this humility we can see clearly that it is the Lord who is at work in all the good that is being done. There is also a special way that the Franciscan life is imparted through the older brothers, whose time-tested faithfulness enflesh the Gospel life. In our relationship with these older brothers, we discover many secrets of our life, which cannot be taught in any other way than by patiently watching, listening, and experiencing their witness of religious life.

— BR. MICHAEL KMIOTEK

The Holy Spirit's work of perfecting charity within us usually comes about in the daily duties of life, as Brother Crispin, shown at work here, reflects.

FRATERNAL LIFE

One of the many great things about our faith is that it takes so very little to please our God. Most of our lives will be spent simply negotiating the turns of everyday life. The daily duties are where the drama of the spiritual life will take place. Most of us imitate our Savior's Passion in situations that are not very passion-inspiring.

This holds true in community life, as well. The consecrated life of a friar includes the lifelong quest to plumb the depths of the mystery of God's love; to ascend the lofty heights of contemplation; to be reshaped in God's image on the anvil of sacrifice. It takes us friars to the places "where angels fear to tread": to the desk heaped with unfinished community business, to the dusty workshop, to a fever-hot kitchen stove, to the phone that rings and rings again. Life's great pilgrimage often takes us straight to the busy post office or into rush-hour traffic. And what a blessing it is! Being faithful to the Lord in everyday life is like waltzing with the Spirit, a mysterious unity of body and soul in every twist and shift as the music plays on and on to an uncertain ending. It is where God truly leads one's life, and we in turn are open to receive His love with its many, often changing, faces.

The Lord has given us many brothers in community. For all of us CFRs, serving God means serving our brother "more tenderly than a mother cares for her children in the flesh", as Saint Francis reminds us. Hands-on work is a major part of how we serve both the poor and our brothers of the community. We do as much of our own work as possible (and some that is impossible), with a view to being poor in spirit *and* in fact, but also in order to put the Gospel ideal of fraternal charity into effect in everyday life. The ideal of fraternal charity is the inspiration and genesis of so much of our lives as friars who are dedicated to renewal. A faithful friar can rightly say with the Lord, "This is my body which is given up for you."

— Br. Crispin Mary Rinaldi

Brother Peter Marie (right) is shown praying with a fellow Englishman, Brother Francis, as they visit a family in Harlem. Brother Peter explains his appreciation of the gift of a lay brother's vocation.

VOCATION OF THE LAY BROTHER

The lay brother's vocation is often hidden and misunderstood. People wonder: Why doesn't he go all the way and become a priest? The simplest answer is that this is the life God has called me to live. It is simply the life of a friar without the added dimension of the ordained ministry, which is a more intense living of the life of Christian perfection. The life of a lay brother is beautiful, full of joy and peace, as is any lived in the full light of Christ. It is a life of prayer, brotherhood, and service, of intimacy and love with the divine Spouse of our soul.

We serve through cooking, questing (begging), cleaning, repairs and maintenance; also through evangelization, especially on a one-to-one basis, and working with the poor in our neighborhoods. One of the great blessings for us is to visit families in their homes. I remember visiting a single mother, whom we met as she was going into an abortion clinic but who, through God's grace, later chose to keep her baby. We would visit her and her children and bring them some groceries and also some devotional pictures to hang in their home. Whenever we visited, we encouraged them to practice their Faith, especially by going to Mass, and we prayed with them (usually, a part of a Rosary).

Traditionally, friars went out in twos—a priest and a lay brother. What a great witness! While the priest preached, the brother quietly prayed and interceded for him that his words would touch the hearts of those listening. Saint Francis once told a preaching friar that more souls were saved by the brother's prayers than by the preacher's words. The brother assisted at Holy Mass and led the faithful in prayer and in examining their consciences while confessions were being heard. This has truly been our experience, as it was for the many Capuchin lay brother saints and blesseds of the past.

Many young men feel a call to religious life but not to the priesthood. The Lord is calling, so we must encourage them to respond with an undivided heart.

— BR. PETER MARIE WESTALL

Brother Paulus Maria is shown drawing a Madonna and Child on the street during a block party in the Bronx. Friars come from many different backgrounds and bring with them a diversity of gifts of the Holy Spirit "for building up the body of Christ" (Ephesians 4:12). Brother Paulus explains.

ART

When I was growing up, in Pirna, near Dresden in East Germany, art was an unbroken thread in my life. Art had a long and glorious history in Saxony and was never seen as the luxury of the few. By the time I was in kindergarten, I began to draw and paint. After I had taken lessons with a fine Dresden painter, my hobby became a profession, and I studied to be a sculptor at the oldest European porcelain studio, in Meissen. I later studied modern art in order to serve as an art teacher at the Franciscan College near Frankfurt.

At the same time, God was shaping my vocation to the Franciscan Order, and I had to become like soft clay in the Creator's hand. I had to learn the art of prayer.

Everything changed when I joined the Franciscan Friars of the Renewal. During my first interview, Father Benedict told me: "We are not a community of artists." Now, however, I see that we are in one sense a community of artists indeed. We restore the oft-hidden beauty of God in the suffering faces, hearts, and souls of our neighbors in the South Bronx.

Following the holy example of Teresa of Calcutta, we may be called to do "something beautiful for God" in the ghetto.

— Br. Paulus Maria Tautz

Brother Francis, shown working on his painting of Pope John Paul II, is a 6-foot-8-inch friar, from East London, who discovered a "latent" gift of the Holy Spirit after a number of years in our community. He reminds us how powerful this gift can be.

ART

What a gift to be able to do something beautiful for God! How much more beautiful is God's gift in sending us His only Son! It was the Incarnation of Jesus Christ that made art acceptable among the early Christians. When God became man, it was possible to have an image of Him. Thank God for that, because my conversion came about when I found a picture of Jesus in a phone booth.

Art is extremely important, and also a powerful way to spread the Gospel. That is why Satan has distorted and corrupted it so much in our time. The media know how effective art is, especially when it shocks and offends.

What we need today is a bold and lively revival of sacred and beautiful art. Deep down, that's what everybody wants from artists. So-called "modern" art just makes me ill! But I love this painting of Pope John Paul II, because it captures his strength and confidence. He was a man of many great gifts, which he never hesitated to use for God's glory. May we all learn from his example!

— BR. FRANCIS EDKINS

*The name of our community, Franciscans of the Renewal, is translated into Spanish as "Franciscanos de la Renovación".
This is very appropriate because the buildings we are allowed to use often require structural "renovations".
The Lord sent us a "bricky" from England, Brother Benedict Joseph, with the gifts necessary for this work,
a work dear to the heart of Saint Francis.*

MANUAL SKILLS

Before I became a Franciscan friar, I had worked all over Europe as a bricklayer. Growing up in Manchester, England, I knew many priests but had never felt the call to priesthood. Now that I am a lay brother, I understand my vocation more and more; and even though a brother cannot offer the Eucharistic sacrifice or hear confessions, he can imitate the Lord's sacrifice through humble service to God and his brothers.

As time has passed, living as a religious brother, I praise God for my ability to work and for the grace to use my hands for God's glory. Pope John Paul II often spoke of achieving fulfillment through manual labor and becoming more fully human through our work. He also emphasized the importance of work to the dignity of the human person.

Making all my work a prayer has become so much a part of my life that I try to do whatever task is given me to the best of my ability, through the grace God has given me, for His never-ending glory.

— BR. BENEDICT JOSEPH DELARMI

MUSIC

Music has always been an important part of my life, from the time I was a choirboy in school and into my adult life. I had various music-related jobs, including playing piano in bars and teaching at inner-city elementary schools; and by profession I was a piano tuner.

Music has played an important role in my life of faith, too, and I have found many ways to be creative musically in worshiping God. Music is very much a part of the friars' life, whether it is singing during the recitation of the Divine Office, a solemn liturgy at a community celebration, or a time of praise and worship during a parish mission or youth retreat. The broad variety of musical traditions and styles reflects the catholicity of our community.

I have often experienced the power of music to pierce hearts and to raise the human spirit to worship God. Once, at a parish mission, a man was about to leave the church after the homily. The brothers began to play their music, and the man stopped to listen. That evening he went to confession—after having been away from the sacrament for many years—and told the priest he had decided to remain in the church because he felt drawn to the music.

The psalmist's words perfectly express the friars' approach to worship through music: "It is good to give thanks to the Lord, to sing praises to thy name, O Most High. . . . For thou, O Lord, hast made me glad by thy work; at the works of thy hands I sing for joy" (Psalm 92:1, 4).

— BR. JOHN BOSCO MILLS

It is no surprise that the Poverello's love for singing in the hills of Umbria has continued to reverberate in his brothers and sisters over the centuries. Brother John Bosco (top) and Brother Solanus (bottom) make use of their musical gifts.

Brother John Bosco writes on this theme.

SACRED MUSIC

*L*et *my prayer be counted as incense before thee, and the lifting up of my hands as an evening sacrifice* (Psalm 141:2). The image of incense wafting toward the ceiling is often used to describe the way Gregorian chant should be sung. There is a sense of effortlessness, or rising up, which is common to all sacred music. This upward movement gently draws the listener's soul higher. It is to help the listener experience more profoundly the great mystery, made present in the liturgy, that sacred texts and actions are clothed in music. In celebration of Holy Mass, God comes down to us, while music is employed to raise us up to Him.

The beauty of Saint Francis's life embodied the ideal effect of sacred music. He was by no means a physically attractive person. Rather, his beauty shone in his actions, words, smile, and at times in his song. It was not through coercion or with "wise argumentation" but through the beauty and sanctity of his life that Francis attracted many to Jesus. Likewise, sacred music does not try to convince; it woos. It communicates the sweet truth of God's love to the human heart in ways that reach beyond language or reason.

Through his life, he reflected these realities to all he met. The echo of the eternal is heard in sacred song; through sacred music the transcendent is made immanent. People experience God and touch Him through the sacred and in His saints. In this way the God we cannot see is, in some mysterious way, made tangible.

— BR. FRANCIS MARY ROALDI

Sister Cecilia follows her namesake's gift of music for the Lord.

Brother Francis Mary, pictured here leading the friars' schola (choir), reflects on the power of liturgical music to raise our hearts to heaven.

Father Stan, shown here at a youth gathering in Brazil,
is well known by young people throughout the world for his musical gifts.
He has used his jazz background to develop "Christian rap"
and other contemporary styles. An openness to the Holy Spirit means using every
opportunity to renew the face of the earth, as he explains here.

MUSIC FOR EVANGELIZATION

Along with serving the poor, evangelization is an essential element of the life of our community and of the Church. I see myself as one preaching through music in an effort to bring the Gospel of Jesus to the heart of today's culture. As Pope John Paul II said, "The Gospel lives always in conversation with culture, for the Eternal Word never ceases to be present to the Church and to humanity. If the Church holds back from culture, the Gospel itself falls silent." Alleluia!

— FR. STAN FORTUNA

Brother Christopher (foreground) and Brother Louis make a joyful song during the Polish pilgrimage.

4. The Assumption of Our Lady

"[H]e has . . . exalted those of low degree."

LUKE 1:52

SAINTS

Word spread that the plane had arrived, calling all to assemble to meet the world traveler. Bishops and State officials, the police escort, and the Knights of Columbus color guard all took their assigned positions as the American Airlines jet from Argentina rolled toward the tarmac. A select crew of baggage handlers came forward to receive the precious cargo. A well-packaged but fairly nondescript crate was carefully lowered from the rear of the aircraft. The Carmelite escorts and the airport cargo managers removed the outer casing to reveal the inner treasure. At that moment the rising sun burst through the morning mist, and a bright ray of light shone on the gilded reliquary of the Little Flower. A baggage handler was so moved that he fell to his knees, made the sign of the Cross, and asked a nearby priest to hear his confession of fifteen years. Saint Thérèse of Lisieux had arrived in the United States, and she was already stirring the grace of conversion.

In October 1999, the Franciscan Friars and Sisters of the Renewal had the singular privilege to be among those who welcomed the relics of Saint Thérèse to New York during their "world visit". The pomp and circumstance of the event contrasted with the saint's "little way". Here were the earthly remains of a young woman who died in near obscurity in a small French town in Normandy. This daughter of Carmel is now named a Doctor of the Church and is leading hearts more deeply along her little way to the face of Jesus.

Along with other friars, I was privileged to bear these remains in solemn procession in Saint Patrick's Cathedral, which overflowed with thousands of people devoted to Saint Thérèse. They all hoped for a momentary glimpse of and a brief prayer before her reliquary. The whole evening was filled with profound solemnity and mystery. How could a simple girl have such spiritual significance in the modern world, so given over to secularism?

As Franciscans, lesser brothers and followers of Saint Francis of Assisi, we too long to live a life of humble service in near obscurity. As men of the Gospel and sons of the Church, we also long to spend our lives bringing souls to the heart of Christ.

Saint Francis, Saint Thérèse, pray for us!

— FR. BERNARD MARIE MURPHY

Not only are we grateful for the gift of our holy Mother and the communion of saints, but we also rely on their assistance. Father Bernard (front right) explains this photo of him and other friars carrying the relics of Saint Thérèse.

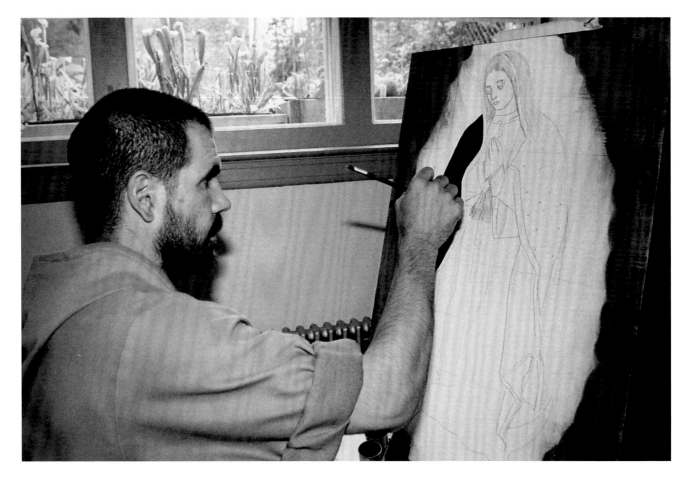

Each of us seeks to become what we contemplate in the life of our Lord and His Mother.
Brother Daniel Marie, shown here, reminds us of the trust and patience needed along this path.

5. The Coronation of Our Lady

"[A] great portent appeared in heaven, a woman clothed with the sun . . ."

REVELATION 12:1

SPIRITUAL GROWTH

Painting an icon of Our Lady of Guadalupe has been both a challenge and a grace-filled experience. It is always a blessing to be able to use a God-given gift to do something in order to give Him glory and to honor His Mother.

The challenge is in trying to reproduce an image that is simple in some ways, but also mystical, for it was miraculously painted by the hand of God. Often the simplest things are the hardest to duplicate, and reproducing the image of Our Lady of Guadalupe is no exception. It is this same challenge we face when we try to grow in holiness. We have before us the example of our Lord or His Mother, yet how often we fall short in our efforts to reproduce it in our lives.

In my struggle to paint, God has taught me to be a little more patient with myself and to accept imperfections, whether on canvas or in my life. This is the great grace we receive only when we pray. All the events of our life begin to speak to us of God and in some way lead us to Him. It doesn't matter whether we have great talent or, seemingly, none. When we entrust what we have to Him, He can make something beautiful out of it—and He desires to do just that.

— BR. DANIEL MARIE WILLIAMSON

*Brother Lawrence and Brother Emmanuel (top) distribute Rosaries in the Bronx,
while Brother Samuel teaches the prayer to boys at Children's Village.
Brother Samuel has experienced the gentle aid of the Queen of Heaven
and here shares his experience of the benefits of the Rosary.*

TEACHING THE ROSARY

Throughout my childhood, our family regularly prayed the Rosary together. This beautiful practice somehow faded away; yet, at about the age of twenty, I felt a greater need for prayer within me. By the grace of God, I could pray the Rosary.

Prayer time is part of religion class on Monday evenings, when the novices of our community visit the Catholic children living in the various cottages of Children's Village, an orphanage in Dobbs Ferry, New York. Prayer with the children commonly includes the Rosary. I pray that the boys of Children's Village will also remember how to say the Rosary as they progress on their journey to the Father.

The *Catechism of the Catholic Church* (no. 971) recalls the words of Pope Paul VI encouraging our Marian devotion and our praying to her: "The Church's devotion to the Blessed Virgin is intrinsic to Christian worship" (*Marialis cultus*, no. 56); and the Rosary itself is an "epitome of the whole Gospel" (no. 42).

— BR. SAMUEL NIX

Sister Lucille, the Community Servant of the Franciscan Sisters of the Renewal,
shown in the chapel of Our Lady of Guadalupe Convent,
speaks about our Lady's faithful assistance.

"And blessed is she who believed that there would be a fulfilment of what was spoken to her from the Lord."

LUKE 1:45

THE ROSARY—MY LIFESAVER

I cannot think of any prayer that has sustained me more than the Rosary, all the days of my life. At a very hard time in my life, when I was in my late twenties, I remember going to a Franciscan priest and sharing my difficulties with him. After listening to me, he gave me a quick solution. He said with a smile, "That's easy. Just pray the Rosary." I did, and it worked!

In days of severe illness or trial, when trauma made praying almost impossible, the Rosary was the only thing that seemed to sustain me. When words would not come, I merely held tight to my rosary beads. Clinging to the beads seemed to *be* my prayer: "Jesus, Mary, I am with you. Help me!" By staying close to the Blessed Mother, I could not fail to receive her help. How could she not keep me close to my beloved Savior with His saving grace?

The words of Saint Jeanne Jugan ring so true: "The Hail Mary will, indeed, take us to heaven."

— SR. LUCILLE CUTRONE

CONTACT INFORMATION

For information on the Friars or Sisters of the Renewal,
go to their Website www.franciscanfriars.com
or
write to:

Franciscan Friars of the Renewal
St. Crispin's Friary
420 East 156 Street
Bronx, NY 10455

Franciscan Sisters of the Renewal
Convent of San Damiano
1661 Haight Avenue
Bronx, NY 10461

For vocational information:

Vocation Director
St. Joseph's Friary
523 West 142 Street
New York, NY 10031

The Friars of the Renewal in England:

St. Fidelis's Friary
Killip Close
London E16 1LX
U.K.

The Friars of the Renewal in Honduras:

Convento San Serafin
Colonia Francisco Morazán
Comayagua
Honduras
C.A.